What Others Are Saying about
Paradox and Pastor Sergio De La Mora...

"My friend, Sergio, has a gift for 'unlimiting' people! His new book helps us untie God's hands so they can work in our life. Get ready to go to another level."

—*Bishop Dale C. Bronner, D. Min.*
Senior pastor, Word of Faith Family Worship Cathedral
Atlanta, GA
Author, *Power Principles*

"Sergio De La Mora in *Paradox* does a brilliant and profound job in both challenging our incorrect views while taking us on a biblical journey of discovering God at a deeper level. There is a freedom we receive when we clearly see God for who He is. The Father is longing to reveal Himself to us so that we can know Him and His nature at a deeper level. Every area in our lives that has embraced an incorrect view of God must be challenged. We must begin to see Him correctly if we are to experience the freedom Jesus paid a great price for. God is excessive in His love for you, extravagant in His forgiveness toward you, and outrageous in His grace to you. Sergio writes from a place of authority that will cause a shift in your life because this is a message he lives out and has been radically transformed by."

—*Banning Liebscher*
Jesus Culture Founder and Pastor

"With his lifelong experience of planting churches and sharing Jesus beyond borders, Pastor Sergio is a true visionary with eyes to see past the rules and limits we often place on God. *Paradox* will stretch your understanding of *who* God is and demonstrate *how* God breaks through barriers to transform our lives. For anyone feeling stuck or constricted or who is questioning their understanding of God—this book is for you!"

—*Chad Veach*
Lead pastor, Zoe Church
Los Angeles, CA

"*Paradox* is riveting! Honestly, I've always loved Sergio De La Mora's teaching, but this book took it a step further by challenging me to quit living a limited life and begin to see God as He sees me...*limitless!*"

—*Bil Cornelius*
Best-selling author
Pastor, Church Unlimited

"Often I have shook my head and said, 'I don't get it. It doesn't make sense. How can it be?' And yet, it is! I am talking about the mystery that my friend Pastor Sergio De La Mora unpacks in his book *Paradox*: that God broke the rules for you. We are all a living paradox—you don't have to understand it, just bask in it and celebrate His grace."

—*Sam Chand*
Leadership consultant
Author, *Bigger Faster Leadership*

"A paradoxical book by a paradoxical leader. I'm honored to know this man and own this book. *Paradox* navigates through the truth of the gospel to reveal the God grace leads us to encounter. Read this book—and learn from one of the best."

—*Chris Durso*
Author, *The Heist: How Grace Robs Us of Our Shame*

"My friend, Sergio, has written a paradigm-changing masterpiece that is an unorthodox merge of head and heart. One of the most insightful books I have ever read. Answering the honest questions we've all asked about God, *Paradox* creates a conversation between readers and God that is heart-revealing, thought-provoking, and life-changing. The more I read, the more I discovered the God who breaks the rules."

—*Benny Perez*
Lead pastor, The Church LV
Henderson, NV

"If you're ready to break the status quo, disrupt legalistic beliefs, and over-throw common misconceptions about God, this is the book you need! Unequivocally one of the best books written by a man who has lived a life marked by broken rules of favor and promotion. Every chapter is biblically accurate, historically accountable, and culturally insightful. It's impossible to read this book and see God the same way."

—*Samuel Rodriguez*
President, National Hispanic Christian Leadership Coalition
Author, *Be Light*

"We have always intuitively known that we must be missing something when it comes to understanding God. This book is by far the strongest argument yet against the mundane Christianity that has plagued our culture. Sergio speaks into a new dimension of relationship with God that dismantles prior misinterpretations of Him. *Paradox* is one of the most important contributions to the church today!"

—*Miles McPherson*
Lead pastor, The Rock Church
San Diego, CA

"Pastor Sergio loves people and he loves Jesus. This book reflects these two factors, and I know it will be a blessing to anybody who reads it. When I think of "paradox," I think of the gospel message that impacts everybody, from a palace filled with well-known people, to a prison perhaps filled with forgotten people. Sergio covers the whole spectrum with his life and I'm glad he's written a book around this concept because we need more people who are willing 'to break some rules.' There is a reason why this pastor has such a multi-cultural and multi-generational impact and I'm excited to see how many lives this book can influence."

—*Carl Lentz*
Lead pastor, Hillsong NYC

"Pastor Sergio has revealed the truth that God never meant for rules to rule our lives. In fact, He's a wild, paradoxical rule-breaker who still knows how to get water out of a rock and finances out of fishes. It's not fair…it's favor! But God continues to break the rules for us…faults and all!"

—David Crank
Senior pastor, FaithChurch
St. Louis, MO, and West Palm Beach, FL

"In life, there are rules and principles that, if we follow them, will benefit us. But Jesus warned the religious leaders of His day about the 'limiting rules' they imposed on people, saying, 'Your traditions have made the Word of God of no effect.' (See Mark 7:13.) Pastor Sergio De La Mora's newest book, *Paradox*, unlocks fresh insight into limiting rules that have bound people and wrongly defined the God of grace, mercy, and power. *Paradox* will help anyone rediscover 'the God beyond the rules' by offering a deeper understanding that will fill them with confidence to step beyond the box of containment and live out the life Jesus paid so dear a price for us to experience."

—Pastors Art and Kuna Sepúlveda
Word of Life Christian Center
Honolulu, HI

"This book will be the game changer in your relationship with God! Every pastor needs to read this, and then read it again and again!"

—Obed Martinez
Lead pastor, Destiny Church
Founder, Passionate Pastor's Network

"*Paradox* is fantastic and a must-read for everyone who wants to be used by God. Sergio De La Mora delivers real insights about how far God is willing to go to 'break the rules' to have a relationship with you. Each chapter reveals practical ways in which God wants to rewrite your rules and bring you back to Him. You do not want to miss out on Sergio's revelation of God's authority over all man-made, hindering rules."

—Dave Minton
Pastor, Capital Christian
Lacey, OR

PAR·A·DOX

THE GOD WHO BREAKS

THE RULES

SERGIO DE LA MORA

WHITAKER
HOUSE

Paradox:
The God Who Breaks the Rules

Sergiodelamora.com

ISBN: 978-1-62911-937-3
International Trade Paperback ISBN: 978-1-62911-973-1
eBook ISBN: 978-1-62911-938-0
Printed in the United States of America
© 2017 by Sergio De La Mora

Whitaker House
1030 Hunt Valley Circle
New Kensington, PA 15068
www.whitakerhouse.com

Library of Congress Cataloging-in-Publication Data

Names: De La Mora, Sergio, 1966– author.
Title: Paradox : the god who breaks the rules / Sergio De La Mora.
Description: New Kensington, PA : Whitaker House, 2017. |
Identifiers: LCCN 2017033403 (print) | LCCN 2017036801 (ebook) | ISBN 9781629119380 (ebook) | ISBN 9781629119373 (trade pbk. : alk. paper)
Subjects: LCSH: God (Christianity)
Classification: LCC BT103 (ebook) | LCC BT103 .D4 2017 (print) | DDC 231.7—dc23
LC record available at https://lccn.loc.gov/2017033403

1 2 3 4 5 6 7 8 9 10 11 ⨄ 24 23 22 21 20 19 18 17

PAR·A·DOX

/ˈperəˌdäks/ noun

a seemingly absurd or self-contradictory statement
or proposition that when investigated or explained
may prove to be well founded or true.

This book is dedicated in loving memory to my mother, Soledad Sanchez De La Mora, who joined my father in heaven as I began writing its beginning chapters. Every word and every thought on these pages is a testament to her unwavering voice in my life that will live on forever. All that I aspire to be and accomplish was first birthed in the prayers and dreams my mother carried in her heart. She was my life-giver, dream-releaser, and truth-teller, and without her guidance and support, all of this could never have happened. *I love you, Chuchi!*

There are many virtuous and capable women in the world,
but you surpass them all!
(Proverbs 31:29 NLT)

CONTENTS

FOREWORD

I met Sergio De La Mora while on a trip to South America. It was Medellin, Columbia, to be precise. We were there with perhaps 10,000 pastors and leaders from Latin America.

What was once the epicenter of the world's most notorious drug cartel was now the gathering place for one of the world's most powerful movements.

The church is alive and well in a part of the world where poverty and violence has marked its history.

This was a profound marker in my life.

This is my world.

These are my people.

Their blood flows through my veins.

You see, I was born in San Salvador, El Salvador. My story begins in the world's most violent city.

Yet, though Spanish was my first language, English had become my primary language. It was both humiliating and frustrating to me that I was speaking with a translator.

It's not that I couldn't speak Spanish, it's that I wouldn't.

Again, it was there that I met Sergio.

When we happened to meet together to share a meal, he revealed to me he went to Medellin so that we might meet. This is somewhat ironic since he lives in San Diego and I live in Los Angeles. I'm sure we had passed by each other in the past, but it was here our lives merged together.

It was in South America that we became partners in crime.

Now that I know him, I'm surprised it took so long for us to connect.

It was there he challenged me to get past my fear and sense of inadequacy about speaking in Spanish and take ownership of my heritage.

It was there that he called me out to own who I was and become the voice our people needed.

He spoke both prophetically and passionately.

I now know this is what Sergio De La Mora does.

He sees greatness in people and calls it out.

He sees past their brokenness and into their potential.

He calls people out and up.

He did the same thing the first time he met my wife, Kim. He looked at her and spoke into her life. He spoke into her fears and spoke into her courage. It really upset her. She told him, "You don't know me!"

That was the paradox.

He didn't know her, but knew her so well she felt unnerved by it.

Sergio sees broken things and is moved to make them new.

He reclaims that which has been discarded.

He finds value where others see none.

Sergio is a surprising man. Though he has had great success, he describes himself as being at the beginning of his journey. He is by all accounts highly accomplished, but is determined, even desperate, to change and grow. He knows himself and is comfortable with himself, but is also committed to reinventing himself.

He is both an artist and an entrepreneur.

He is practical and poetic.

He is always talking about breaking the rules.

He is breaking his own rules.

He is throwing all his past success on the altar and offering it as a sacrifice to the future.

He is a paradox.

He has thrived in tradition and thirsts for innovation.

He is a Mexican American from Santa Barbara, California.

The son of a millionaire who cares for the poor.

A landscape architect who aspires to be a cultural architect.

A former skateboarder who feels as comfortable on the streets as he does on the stage.

A former DJ who understands the power of music to reach the heart and shape a culture.

He's a successful businessman and the senior pastor of one of America's fastest growing churches.

He lives and serves at the intersection of Chula Vista—one of the most affluent areas of San Diego—and National City—one of the poorest.

He leads both the rich and the poor, the educated and uneducated.

Befitting a Hispanic, he uses a language of revolution, but it's a heart revolution.

I love how Sergio fights for people.

I love the courage he shows when he pursues a vision.

I love how loyal he is to his friends even when they do not merit it.

I love how every square foot of his home and yard has a story behind it, rich with meaning and metaphor.

I love that after all these years he is still passionately in love with Jesus and with people.

You would think I met Sergio at the end of his journey since fifty years have passed, but I'm convinced I have met him at the beginning.

Of this I am certain.

The best is yet to come.

Though the past has been glorious.

He leaves it behind for the future.

That's the paradox.

That's Sergio De La Mora.

Forward,
Erwin Raphael McManus

Lead Pastor, Mosaic, Los Angeles
Author, *The Last Arrow*

The last shall be made first, and the first, last.

1

REDEFINING GOD

"You are remembered for the rules you break."
—Douglas MacArthur

This book is about change.

Not about changing God, but changing how we see Him and, more importantly, how we let Him see us.

Let's be honest: the hardest thing to admit is when we're wrong, but sometimes, we're just wrong. The ideas, perspectives, and stances that come flowing through the filter of "religious rules" have often—painfully often—painted the wrong picture of God. So wrong, that when we finally somehow hear the truth about God, it sounds unbelievable. Absurd. Contradictory.

Most of the people I've talked to who have walked away from God would say it's because of a set of rules they could never live up to—rules that became the standard or the status quo that they just couldn't follow.

Not because they didn't want to. Not because they didn't desire to adhere to the standards set before them. And not because they didn't understand the consequences of abandoning the path marked out for them. Rather, it was because the standards, the rules, gave no room to grow, learn, and succeed from areas of weakness, past mistakes, or imperfections.

And so they walked away from the inner vows they'd made to follow God because they simply couldn't walk out the outer vows they'd made to religious rules. The weight of discouragement and guilt over the things they *weren't* doing right took precedence over the things they *were* doing right until, eventually, it seemed pointless to keep trying.

For many, following God feels like a 16-wheel semi-truck trying to drive on a narrow bike lane. There just isn't any room for mistakes. We try to convince ourselves that we can walk a perfect line for a while, but it's only a matter of time before we end up losing our balance and falling over. A boxed-in life with no opportunity to learn through trial and error is not only unfathomable, it's unsustainable. The tightrope walk of rule-abiding perfection isn't the kind of life any of us want to live. More importantly, it's not the life God *intended* for us to live. It's a great misconception about God that He wants us to live perfectly. Despite what we've been told, God never meant for rules to rule our lives.

In fact, I want to introduce you to a paradox—an idea, notion, and thought about God that seems absurd, contradictory, absolutely not possible. Even, to some, blasphemous. Or humorous. So once you're done arguing, laughing, and doubting, I would like to introduce you to Someone you may not truly know.

I want to introduce you to a God who breaks the rules.

UNORTHODOX METHODS

I heard a story once about America that I never learned in school. Around the time of the Revolutionary War, many people were convinced America was anything but great. They believed America was populated with people and animals of lesser intelligence, lesser strength, and lesser ability and was doomed to failure. The idea, so ridiculous to our ears now, came from a popular, massive encyclopedia of natural history, *Histoire Naturelle*, written by the French nobleman Count Georges-Louis Leclerc Buffon. Although Buffon had never actually traveled to America, he was absolutely convinced of its inevitable decline and collapse because, he wrote, the dense forests and marshes made it impossible for anyone or anything to develop properly. Hundreds of thousands of people believed him—and were too scared to try to make a life in a new land.

Buffon's encyclopedia, of course, was a huge public relations crisis for the brand-new United States of America. In order to survive, the US desperately needed high immigration and a flourishing trade industry. It needed proof that its land was not degenerate and diseased but full of life and opportunity.

One man in particular took it upon himself to set the world right: Thomas Jefferson. He knew he had to do something drastic, even unorthodox, to turn the perception around.

Living in France at the time, Jefferson pleaded with his friends in America to hunt, shoot, preserve, stuff, and send a gigantic moose all the way across the ocean to Buffon as tangible proof of America's grandiose wilderness and vast resources. Jefferson asked for a moose big enough to make every other European animal pale in comparison and show that Buffon was as foolish as his encyclopedia. Sending a beast as grand in size and mass as a moose would prove once and for all that America was not only viable and fertile, but also far superior. When the massive seven-foot-tall stuffed moose eventually arrived on his doorstep, the French scientist couldn't deny that his notions about America were wrong. Buffon was convinced, and Jefferson's radical step began the unraveling of an idea that could have proved fatal to the nascent United States. And Jefferson changed America's future in the raw, muddy wilderness at the hands of brute hunters instead of through the articulate, intelligent discussions of enlightened men of position and power.

What if I were to tell you God did the same thing Jefferson did, just hundreds of years before? I'm not sure of His exact height, but, in essence, Jesus was the seven-foot-tall moose who was sent to change some widespread but incorrect beliefs about God.

And as theologically irrational as it may seem, God has always been set on challenging, frustrating, and unnerving people's precepts through unorthodox methods. For a man named Moses, God broke the rules of nature to part the Red Sea. For a man named Joshua, He broke the rules of astronomy to stop time in the middle of a crucial battle. For a woman named Rahab, He broke societal rules to include her in the lineage of Jesus. For a man named Saul, later called Paul, He broke religious rules to intervene and dramatically change a man on the wrong mission. For a young teenage couple named Joseph and Mary, God broke personal rules to birth His Son through this virgin.

Even back then, God was not afraid to break the rules to accomplish change. And just so today, He will still use some of the most unorthodox methods to convince us of the truth. Time and time again, we think, "It can't be done this way." But God says, "It *can*." God doesn't change and neither does His Word. But His methods of reaching us are constantly changing. An unchanging God who changes or breaks the rules to meet us is an absurdity and a contradiction—but it is, in fact, true.

It's a paradox.

You are one of the rebels, rule-breakers, and radicals of today who embody the very definition of greatness.

Like Jefferson, so many of us know what crazy, unorthodox plan we need to take. So why, if we know what it takes, do we not take the brazen risks to achieve what we have only dreamed of? Why do more people seem to be standing outside of the gilded gates of their future than flourishing inside? Why do the pioneers of change we so admire seem to live only in stories of yesterday? Where are the modern-day Thomas Jeffersons, Rosa Parks, Martin Luther King Jrs, Amelia Earharts, Pablo Picassos, and more?

I believe they're in the minds and hearts of people just like you. You're reading a book that by its very title doesn't make sense. You're reading a book about finding the courage to change the unchangeable. You're reading a book about changing the way you see God and your life. You are one of the rebels, rule-breakers, and radicals of today who embody the very definition of greatness.

THE GOD WHO BROKE MY RULES

Now at this point, I should probably tell you I'm a pastor. My job is to help point people to a relationship with God through His Son, Jesus. Some of you may be ready to close these pages simply because I'm a pastor and to walk away from yet another "religious book." But today, right here, I would ask that you give me a chance. As someone who has helped thousands change the course of their life, allow me to be a change specialist for you who introduces you to the God who breaks the rules. Give me a shot at painting a different picture of God than you may currently hold. Walk with me on this journey to discover a God who isn't the rule-keeper most people think He is. Give me permission to show you the God who broke my rules.

You see, I started out as a young kid who followed all of God's rules. My parents were devout Catholics, and I was raised to follow in their footsteps of faith. I was an altar boy who never missed a service. Regardless of what was on our personal schedules, all six of the De La Mora children were expected to attend mass together. I knew *of* God but I had very little relationship *with* Him personally. To me, God was rigid, linear, and unwavering in His rules. I felt He was stoic and apathetic to my personal pains, looking only to punish me for my wrongdoings. Every ritual and sacrament intended to draw me closer to God eventually pushed me farther away—not because I felt God was disappointed by me, but because of my own guilt of disappointing Him.

On the outside, I upheld my responsibilities as an altar boy, but I lacked the richness of relationship I saw in my parents' closeness with God. They seemed undeterred by the vast rules and stipulations of religion. It was as though their generation seemed content to obey without a hunger and passion for *more* from God. I felt guilty every time I broke a rule, but I had no idea how to change.

Inside, I knew I needed this distant God to change for me, but I knew that was too absurd to ask. Here I was struggling with too many secret sins to count, including a cocaine habit. Why would God change His rules for someone like me? It didn't seem possible.

At seventeen, I had my own successful DJ company and was about to sign a seven-year record contract. But then I had a dream that changed everything. In my dream, I was standing at a fork in the road with two signs in front of me: one read "worldly success" and the other, "ministry." I heard God's voice say to me, "If you sign that contract, you'll have success, but you'll miss the purpose for your life. Sergio, follow Me."

At that time, I was a far cry from a man qualified for ministry. That dream had to be a mistake! It just didn't add up. God would definitely be looking for someone who was rule-*abiding*, not rule-*breaking*. The God I knew would never personally speak to a sinner like me! Where in my dream was the priest who served as the middle man between God's holiness and my dirtiness? Where was my list of penances to perform before I could be clean enough to be good enough? Where was the angry face of a God who didn't care about my struggles?

Despite what I thought I knew about God, all I felt was God's invitation to know Him differently.

Today, the God I know is engaged, forgiving, and evident in my life. He speaks to the depths of my heart and leads me where He wants me to go rather than where I'm qualified to go. He opens doors of influence that were at one time closed to me and my family. He breaks the opinions, perspectives, and judgments others have of me, and those that I have of myself, to reveal His merciful viewpoint. When I stumble in my journey to understand Him better, He stands with arms wide open instead of turning His back in disdain and disappointment. He erases the lines that separate me from Him and draws with broader, bigger strokes that include my weaknesses, faults, and inconsistencies.

Over the years, I've often thought back on that young man at seventeen and reflected on how differently I see God now. I've realized that it wasn't God who had changed; it was me who had changed. It was my image, my understanding, and my rules that had changed. I allowed God to break the rules in me that I had inadvertently given permission to reign over me. The rules that had tormented me with guilt began to change as I sought out a relationship with Him as a son instead of through religion.

The course of my life has not been one that reflects a journey of perfect, rule-abiding choices and decisions. It's been a walk of grace that has journeyed to a deeper, richer, and wider road without the stagnant rules I once held about God.

And the rules in me weren't the only rules God broke. As I trusted Him more and more and enlarged my perspective of Him, He began to break cultural, societal, and religious rules for me as well. I am the classic example of a man with no formal training who was found by God, changed by God, and is now being powerfully used by God in ways only few would ever have imagined possible!

After over three decades of walking with God, I've realized God is not just the God who makes the rules. He's also the God who will *break the rules* for you. I realize the idea of a pastor emboldening people to believe in a God who breaks rules is quite the paradox, but the God I've come to know isn't afraid of breaking the rules to help us change what seems unchangeable. He Himself isn't beyond breaking some rules on our behalf.

BLASPHEMY?

But why? Why would God want to break the rules? Wouldn't He want the opposite? Isn't God a rule-keeper, not a rule-breaker?

In the mind of humanity, we think of rules as "good" and breaking them as "bad." This is why rule-breaking is synonymous with negative words such as *defiance* and *rebellion*. God's perspective, however, is different. He doesn't desire the abolishment of rules; He desires the destruction of any and all barriers that keep us from knowing Him and truly living the life He created us to live.

As a seventeen-year-old boy, David was really nothing more than a soiled field worker. His own family saw no greatness in David, and his brothers looked at him as an arrogant troublemaker. He was far from a king, far from a leader, far from promotion, but because he wasn't far from God, nothing could stop him.

His inauguration was not exactly what you'd expect for the next king. It was actually a secret venture under false pretenses, a deception that God permitted. No one expected David to be the leader that he would eventually become. He had the wrong qualifications, wrong family lineage, and wrong reputation. Everything about David seemed wrong, but to God, everything about David was right. God saw a man whose heart belonged to Him.

And because God decided to promote him, David's life was a continual paradox. From the moment God called him, rules were broken. Over the course of his life, David would go on to become one of the greatest leaders, even though he made mistake after mistake. Although God privileged David, He didn't overlook David's actions. God didn't give David the green light to do whatever he wanted, but He did use his life as an example to say, "Let Me change how you see Me so you can see *all of Me.*"

God is met in the pages of His Word and the being of His Son, not in a set of rules.

While the idea of God being a "rule-breaker" may seem outrageous, believing God would break rules on our behalf—personally and individually—is likely even more absurd. Throughout the course of this book, we'll use David's life to look at the reasons why God broke the rules and how He wants to do the same in your life today. God has always wanted relationship, but He won't force relationship, especially if we hold tighter to a system of rules than we do to Him. He'll wait until we're ready to change how we see, think, and understand Him.

Too often an incorrect and traditional image of God leads us to form inward rules about Him, ourselves, and others that skew our perspectives. They speak out with statements such as, "God can't," "God won't," and "God will never." Eventually these inner declarations evolve into, "I can't," "I won't," and "I'll never." Such assertions prevent us from venturing forth and breaking out of fears and self-imposed restrictions in order to s change in the different areas of our life. These hindering, personal limitatic become a prison that locks us into a life we think we're supposed to live.

The irony is that rules were never intended to control people. Th were never created to define God in our lives. Rules were only intended to te standards. But in the centuries since Christ's resurrection, rules have bec synonymous with religion as the image of God was drawn with a paintbr of do's and don'ts. And more and more people pulled away from God ar His plan for their lives. They retreated to the notion that they would rather make up their *own* rules for their life than follow God's.

They had the wrong idea of God.

NEVER WORTHLESS AGAIN

When I first met Anna, she had just gotten out of prison. As a little girl, Anna had gone to church every Sunday and clearly remembered the wonder of a childlike faith to believe for anything. But over the years, out of a sense of guilt and fear, she had chosen to walk away from God. For over twenty years, she had battled an addiction that eventually caused her to lose everything, including her two children. Her confidence and hope in life were cut off and the dreams she once carried of a career in the legal profession were long gone. Her reckless lifestyle had left a mark on her health that was irreversible. Now diagnosed with a terminal disease, she stepped through the doors of our church in search of any trace of the faith she once knew, an empty shell of the woman she once was. I remember looking into her lifeless, dark eyes and coming face to face with the pain that seemed to have no end and no beginning.

All her life she had broken rules that had broken her family, broken her spirit, and broken her future. No matter how much I spoke to her about hope and change, it was evident in her face that she didn't believe I could be talking about *her* life. There were Sundays when I shook her hand and she was sober, and there were Sundays when I shook her hand and she was high. She teetered back and forth in her faith and in her reality as an addict. There were breaks in her weekly attendance when I knew she was too sick, too high, or in too much trouble with the law to come, but we kept praying and believing. Eventually, she always came back.

On Sunday I found out Anna was in the hospital. The doctors had discovered a large mass on her kidney that needed to be removed, but there was no guarantee she would make it through the surgery alive. Doctors feared her body wouldn't have the functionality to survive the surgery, even though it was necessary to remove the mass. It seemed to be a story with an inevitable bad ending. When I visited her at the hospital, Anna looked at me with a face of resignation and defeat. The first words she said to me were, "This is my punishment. I'm getting what I deserve." She seemed resolved to die whether she went through with the surgery or not. It was brutally painful to try and convince her that God could still change her story. Her biggest argument was, "*Why?*" Why would God want to save someone like her when she obviously had done everything but follow Him? She argued with me that though she believed God *could*, she fiercely doubted He *would*. With every fiber of her being, she felt unqualified, undeserving, and unworthy of a miracle. Tears rolling down her face, she looked around the empty hospital room and wondered aloud how God could ever show up for her when even her own family hadn't. I prayed with her that night, and then left for home. I cried the entire way home, knowing what she was feeling, but unable to convince her otherwise. A young pastor at the time, it was the longest car ride of my life.

A few days later, I returned to the hospital to check on Anna. Her room was dark, and the bed was empty. Fearing the worst, I asked the nurses what had happened. They said Anna had just been released, but without a way to get a hold of Anna, I wasn't sure what to think, so I just kept praying. Two Sundays later, I watched as Anna gingerly and cautiously walked up the stairs that led to our services. Her eyes were tired and worn, but I saw something there I hadn't seen before. There was *life* in her eyes. I reached out and hugged her, unsure of what to ask or say. She slowly smiled and said two words: "It's gone." Speechless, I began to express gratitude at her successful surgery but she quickly stopped me. "I didn't have surgery. The mass is just gone. It disappeared. They can't find it anymore." The doctors couldn't explain it, but I knew God had broken the rules of medical science for this woman.

She didn't say much those first weeks, but her face changed every time I saw her. Her resolve to live got stronger and stronger as she slow began to accept the miracle God had given her. Years later, she came to me a in with that slow smile and said the same words: "It's gone." Incredulous, again stood speechless in front of her. The latest lab results had revealed no longer showed any sign of the terminal disease in her body. Nothing, ot one infected cell. Nada. That was over ten years ago and today she rem a medical miracle. Come on, somebody!

If Anna's story had been one of a dying young child or community philanthropist, it might make more sense why God would break the rules on her behalf. But that God would do so much for someone society deemed "worthless"—it's a paradox!

I thought back then that maybe God saw the woman Anna would become if she could just believe in a God that loved, accepted, and believed in her more than His rules. Then the greatest miracle for Anna would seemingly be a second chance at life physically. But now I would argue for a different perspective: the greatest miracle God gave Anna was not her physical life, but the *faith* to believe in Him in a way that superseded any and every limitation, hindrance, and obstacle. The seeds of faith He planted through her medical miracle grew when her relationship with her children was restored. And it grew even more when God began to use her to speak to other women with similar stories. Then it grew even more when doors of opportunity began to open for jobs that were once slammed in her face because of her past.

In God's eyes, the perfect person to break the rules for is the person who, in our eyes, is the most imperfect.

Years later, she told me she kept coming back to our church because never before had someone made her feel like it didn't matter where she'd been or what she'd done. Knowing my own relationship with God and the rules He had broken for me, I truly believe God broke my rules so I could introduce Anna to the God who would break her rules. The faith that once said God wouldn't do things for her now said God wouldn't stop doing things for her. He wasn't looking for a perfect person to do a perfect miracle. As baffling as it may seem, it's almost as though, in God's eyes, the perfect person to break the rules for is the person who, in our eyes, is the most imperfect.

NGING THE WAY YOU SEE GOD

This thought shakes the core of how we see God. It means that the essence of a relationship with God is not based on merit or adherence to rules, but on faith alone. The fact that God would do crazy and unorthodox miracles for the righteous and unrighteous alike blurs our rigid understanding of God. No longer is it crystal clear whom God will promote, advance, and favor. The rules of engagement are forever changed. Now, God's inclusivity qualifies *all* of us to have our rules broken.

But this all-inclusive life God intended for us is only possible when we allow Him to break the inner rules or vows we've clung to out of tradition and obligation. These inner rules offer little help in conquering the real internal struggles of defeat, disappointment, and discouragement we all face at one time or another. God wants to show you and me that He loves us, accepts us, and wants to favor us, regardless of our merits, works, or even obedience to rules. *He just wants us.* All of us, with every single one of our hang-ups, issues, and mistakes.

The paradox of God's rule-breaking persona is a side of Him we all need.

God broke the rules over two thousand years ago, before any one of us was born, to show us how deeply and greatly He wanted us. He saturated the earth with His grace to eliminate every argument within us that would hinder us from living the life we were called to live. Through these pages, He will reveal who you were called to be, destined to be, regardless of the internal and external vows you've held on to that need to be broken. Not one single rule could change His love and plan for your life centuries ago, and not one single rule can stop it today.

Take a moment and think of the rules you've harbored out of tradition, expectation, or religion. Which rules have you held to for fear of disappointing God, yourself, or others? What "truths" have held you captive from the life you have always longed for? Once you begin to honestly assess your own rulebook, you'll begin to see the rules that now need to be broken. Maybe they're rules about God's love for you. Maybe they're rules about what you are or are not qualified to possess in life. Or maybe it's a set of rules about others that has placed a wall between you and them. Whatever the rules have been, it's time to discover the God who wants to break them.

For those who have never had a relationship with Him, an encounter with this God starts a conversation with Him that is the beginning of a real relationship. It's the starting point to seeing God as real, relevant, and responsive to you personally. It's the blank canvas you need to see Him differently from the rumors you've heard about Him. It's the brand new beginning you've needed, but felt you could never get. It's the thing you've always desired but could never put your finger on.

For those who have had a relationship with God but walked away or struggled to get closer to Him, it's the key to everything you've been trying to unlock. It's the faith truth that overpowers the truth of rules you've struggled with. It's the green light to *go* where you've never been before in order to access things you could only dream of previously. It's the road less traveled that opens your eyes to see the miraculous, the unexplainable, and the inconceivable. No matter where your relationship with God is today, it can change right now. All you have to do is let Him. Whatever belief system, perspectives, and opinions you hold about God at the start of this book will not be the same ones you have at the end of this journey. I believe by the last page, you'll be more convinced than ever before of who He is and who you are to Him.

Allow me to introduce you to the God you may not know. He's the God who created you, formed you, and called you before you ever breathed your first breath. He's the God who isn't angry at you for the things you've done, didn't do, or even the things you *will* do. He's the God who loves you unconditionally, regardless of whether you love Him. He's the One who ordered every day of your life and marked you with gifts, talents, and abilities to fulfill your purpose. And He's the God who broke the rules to know you.

The adulterer and murderer can be the
"man after God's own heart."

2

THE MYSTERY OF GRACE AND TRUTH

Truth makes Grace desirable.
Grace makes Truth responsible.

Today, men and women rarely play only one role. We're parents, bosses, CEOs, athletes, students, friends, mentors, and more—all simultaneously. We move in and out of countless hats during the course of one day. The idea of a person doing only "one thing" is an incomprehensible concept. Like it or not, the more equipped we are to successfully manage duality, the better off we are in life. We are more flexible in this twenty-first-century society than we have ever been before.

So, here's my question: if we expect ourselves and our society to be so flexible, why do we expect our God to be one-faced, one-faceted, and one-purposed?

He isn't just "one thing," either.

Every Christian loves Scriptures like Hebrews 13:8 that tell us Jesus is the same yesterday, today, and forever. Perhaps because modern life proceeds at such a breathless pace, we seem to want, expect, and assume God will remain unchangeable and constant. We want a God without any surprises or plot twists; we want comfort in this ever-changing world that God is the same. The problem with this train of thought is that it takes one thing for granted. It's banking on the belief that what we know of God, Jesus, and Christianity is *everything* there is to know. We're assuming that we see the whole picture and know all the moving pieces. I emphatically believe in the authenticity of Hebrews 13:8, as well as the whole Bible, but I also know I don't know all there is to know about Jesus.

It's this reality that gives God permission to break the rules I held to *yesterday* and introduce new truths *today* that will shape and influence my *tomorrow*. It allows Him to usher in a fuller truth that overshadows the half-truths I understood previously.

I realized that God didn't want a perfect life from me.

When I first became a Christian I believed that God wanted perfection from me. I held tightly to the idea that God would only be pleased with a radical, full conversion that included a no-returns policy on my old life. I was profoundly grateful for the opportunity God had given me to start over with Him, but I felt this immense pressure to make sure I didn't mess it up. See, I was the first in my family to convert from Catholicism to Christianity and everyone was waiting to see if my conversion was legitimate. If I didn't walk any differently, then the grace that brought me into relationship with Jesus wouldn't have been believable.

As I began to understand more of God, however, I realized that God didn't want a perfect life from me. He just wanted to know that I was willing to surrender and let His grace and His truth work in my life.

BOTH/AND

Seeing that our backgrounds and experiences are all different, let's agree to some working definitions for the terms "truth" and "grace" so that we're all on the same page.

Truth is anything that originates and correlates with God's revealed character, authority, will, and existence. In basic terms, truth is the representation of who God is to humanity. If truth were to come from any other place than God, why does every religious quest to interpret truth always lead us back to God? Those who seek truth inevitably bring God to the table for debate because trying to explain or refute truth without talking about Him is like trying to explain breathing without taking a breath. God and truth are inseparable.

Grace, on the other hand, is God's response to our misuse, misunderstanding, and mistreatment of His truth. Grace is undeserved merit at Christ's expense. In basic terms, grace is the representation of God's infinite love to humanity. Truth helps us know who God is while grace helps us understand who we are to Him.

We often throw the term *grace* around as a way to express a pardon for a wrongdoing. It's our way of saying we forgive what was done to us. This definition of grace is actually erroneous! What we're really expressing is mercy, not grace. *Mercy* is the holding back of what one does deserve, while *grace* is receiving what one doesn't deserve. The truest essence of grace speaks more of favor, promotion, and access than pardon or exemption.

The cross paints a picture of mercy and grace that perfectly exemplifies the roles each play in our lives. Our sins earned us the cross and still needed to have a punishment, so mercy had to step in. Mercy held back real, serious, and painful consequences from us, and put them on Christ instead. Then, grace walked out. It was mercy that led Jesus to the cross, but it was His grace that gave us permission to live beyond the cross. Before there could be grace, there first had to be mercy.

Grace never says we don't *deserve* the cross. Rather, grace says we can take Jesus' place next to God because He took our place on the cross. Grace favored and promoted us into a relationship with Him instead of leaving us at the foot of the cross. Mercy covered us and grace promoted us.

When we understand and accept the truth of grace, we begin to see grace not as a free pass out of jail, but instead as a free pass into promotion. What we once regarded as truth has been exposed by a greater truth, in the same way that the truths you held as a young kid have probably changed as you've aged and matured. I doubt any of us still put our lost teeth under our pillow or write a letter to the man at the North Pole in December. In other words, truth according to us is not always the same as truth according to Him. His truth is the greater truth that exposes what we perceive as truth. As He said, *"I am the way and the truth and the life. No one comes to the Father except through me"* (John 14:6 NIV).

Now that may sound cultish or extreme if you don't have a relationship with Him, but remember that truth doesn't just describe God's character, it is His actual person. God is truth, and so knowing truth is hinged on trusting God. While this may seem like a lot to claim, consider this: All of us tie "truth" to "trust" in almost every aspect of our lives. We read books by experts and specialists and accept their findings as truth enough to at least try their methods and approaches to everything from business to parenting. We willingly accept they're the experts, so we trust them and believe that what they're saying is true. We attend institutions of education under the widely accepted premise that we are being taught truth. We accept what's being taught as truth because we trust the one conveying it. If we trust God, we will accept what He says as truth.

On the flip side, we will struggle to accept God's truth if we don't know Him. People who wrestle with accepting God's truth as their personal truth often have limited or no relationship with Him that would warrant trust in Him. But when you and I let God break our rules about truth and grace, we encounter characteristics of God that we would never have known otherwise.

Just take Abraham.

In the book of Genesis, we read about a man who stood for God's truth and was called righteous because of it. He walked along the shore with God and had intimate conversations with Him that we can only dream of having today. He trusted the truth of God's promises with such absolute faith, he was willing to move his family from everything he'd ever known to a land where he was nothing more than a stranger. So deep was Abraham's trust in God's truth that, after all that, when God then asked him to do the *unthinkable*, he willingly obeyed.

Now if you don't know this story, let me explain God's unthinkable request in the most honest way possible: God told Abraham to murder his only son.

What makes this request even more unthinkable is the fact that this was the son who was supposed to be the beginning of a whole new nation! Abraham had been told by God he would be the father of multitudes, that his descendants would eventually be more than the sands on the seashore, starting with this son Isaac. But now here is God telling Abraham to kill the very gift He had promised him. Here is the God who says, "Thou shalt not kill" telling Abraham to kill his son. Unbelievable. Absurd. Contradictory. *How can this be OK to God?* we think. *This is paradoxical!*

I have six daughters and I have to be honest with you, I wouldn't be able to obey a request like that. I wouldn't be able to accept God's direction to murder as truth. I would *want* to follow God's rules, but honestly, I couldn't. So how and why would Abraham do it? The Bible gives us a clue into Abraham's faith: "*Abraham reasoned that if Isaac died, God was able to bring him back to life again*" (Hebrews 11:19).

From where I sit, that's quite a gamble. From where Abraham sat, it must have sounded like any other command from God. That's an incredible amount of trust to have in the truth of God's character! So here's Abraham in Genesis 22 walking up a mountain along with his son, Isaac, who's carrying across his back the wood he'll die on. Abraham builds the altar, ties up his son, and has the knife in the air ready to plunge into Isaac when God intervenes from heaven and tells him to stop. In the thicket is a ram to sacrifice instead.

What blows my mind about this story is that as soon as God shows up on the scene and cancels His incredible command, Abraham's first response is to acknowledge a characteristic of God he didn't know previously. (See Genesis 22:14.) He doesn't erupt in joy or celebration at the life of his son. He doesn't curse God for testing him in such an insane way. No, his first response is to acknowledge a new truth about God and His character. Not the truth he knew at the bottom of the mountain, but a greater truth about the provision of God that he could only find at the top of the mountain. He encounters a revealed truth about God that he couldn't have experienced without coming so close to pain, tragedy, and death.

That day on Mount Moriah, Abraham encountered the *truth* of God's promises. And on that very same mountain thousands of years later, Jesus would die on a cross so we could encounter the *grace* of God's promises. On that mountain, the mystery of truth and grace was revealed.

Regardless of what crossroads you
find yourself in, God wants you to know
He's ready to show up and intervene.

Think back to your own life and to some of the painful, honest crossroads you've known. A moment that brought you face to face with something that you believed to be entirely true, although it made no logical sense. That very moment was and is an opportunity for you to know a new revelation of God in your life that exceeds every previous notion of who you knew Him to be. If that moment came with the belief of a dream that you felt you had to let go of, God wants to show up to be your dream-builder. If that moment happened in a relationship that you walked away from either by choice or by circumstance, there's a relationship-restorer in God that you need to know. If that moment came in a painful experience that turned out completely differently from what you expected, there's a healer in God that exists for your benefit. Regardless of what crossroads you find yourself in, God wants you to know He's ready to show up and intervene. And not just in the typical places, like church or a Bible study. God is ready to show up at work, at school, and at home. He's even ready to show up in a bar, a club, a jail cell, a board room, or a retirement home. Wherever *you* are is where He'll go to show you more of Himself, His grace, and His truth.

If God is all truth to you, grace will be expendable. If God is all grace to you, truth will be insignificant. If you live strictly by what you perceive to be "right," then you will begin to think you are right, and eventually be tempted to put yourself in the place of God. With this perspective, it's only a matter of time before you lose sight of the constant need for grace.

But if you live so convinced that what you do or believe doesn't matter because God's unlimited grace covers all, then you will live without following any guidelines at all. You'll think, *Grace covers everything, so what's the point of rules?* With this perspective, you'll lose sight of the need for God's consistent guiding force of truth in your life.

Both of these perspectives are flawed. The idea behind both of these one-track philosophies is that grace eradicates truth, or vice versa. But we need grace *and* truth. Truth without grace in any area of our life can lead to legalism while grace without truth can lead to antinomianism, or *anti-law*.

Grace cannot exist without truth, and truth cannot exist with grace. There is a union between God's grace—His broad, merciful, favoring love—and His truth—His close, all-seeing, just honesty. If you have a relationship with God, you know that whenever truth shows up, grace comes around the corner too. If you don't have a relationship with Him and have only encountered His truth, grace wants to come around the corner to meet you right where you are, just like it met David.

GRACE OVER GUILT

David was called a man after God's own heart, yet he was also the man who committed adultery and murder. How can these be two sides of the same coin? Because God promoted David, not his sins. He protected David, not his flaws. He privileged David, not his weaknesses. God saw David in spite of David. God saw the truth of David's character and the areas that were still imperfect, but He also saw who David was on the inside. He saw that David genuinely longed to please Him but struggled to live from the truth of that reality. Every time David made a mistake, God reminded him of who he really was, not who his poor choices and decisions told him he was.

Grace worked in David to confront the inconsistencies in him that didn't reflect the real man inside of him while *truth* worked in him to confront his humanity that made him aware of his constant need of God. The king inside David could never have been formed without the help of both truth and grace.

What God can grace *in* you,
He can grace *through* you.

Like David, many of us want to have a relationship with God and follow His rules, but our inconsistencies and independence make us feel like God doesn't see us. However, God sees you in spite of you. His grace and truth work in you to promote you, protect you, and privilege you despite your sins, flaws, and mistakes. Letting God break the rules of truth in you to introduce grace serves as a foundational platform for Him to begin to break every other rule that has limited your belief in Him.

What God can grace *in* you, He can grace *through* you.

For most of us, God's paradoxical love is just hard to believe. Of everybody, God has seen us at our worst. Yet, although He could rightfully punish us for violating His rules over and over again, He instead chooses to break the rules Himself to draw us back to Him. Consider the adulterous woman in the book of John who was scorned and rightly accused of violating Levitical law. We read in Scripture that she walked away unscathed from her condemners because Jesus chose to break the rules for her. (See John 8:1–12.) We are all like this woman in one way or another. Whether it be in public or private, we've all broken rules that would alienate us from God. But just like Jesus demonstrated, God's desire is not to *guilt* us into relationship, but rather to *grace* us into relationship. One of the biggest errors people believe about grace is thinking that it affects what we've done in the past more than who we will become in the future. But just the opposite is true.

NOT A "HAPPILY EVER AFTER"

A couple I met a few years ago walked such a beautiful line of grace and truth that I never forgot their story. Nathan was in his late twenties when he started coming to our church. He was an exceptional student on the road to a successful medical career. For three years, he volunteered any time he had outside of his work and school to helping our community. He was always eager to ask questions and learn how to improve himself, and he would pick the brain of every leader to figure out the keys behind their success. His even temperament was well-liked and respected among those he followed and those who followed him.

Well-mannered and polite, Nathan, I knew, wouldn't remain single for too long in our church. One day he met her—Nicole. But instead of dating her the typical way everyone expected, Nathan asked her to take premarital classes with him. It was unorthodox, unconventional, and unheard-of. His reasoning was that he'd rather know ahead of the game if it was going to work with her than spend months guessing through traditional dating. Some of his peers thought he was crazy while others admired his nobility. But no one could doubt that it worked. They fell in love and in less than a year, they got married. Grace had handed him a beautiful wife in Nicole, who loved, admired, and understood his unorthodox ways.

You're probably expecting me to tell you they lived happily ever after. That's not entirely accurate. The truth is Nathan could be just as selfish as he was selfless, as angry as he was tranquil, and as immature as he was mature. In work, friends, and community, he could pick and choose the moments that kept him in the lane of grace. But marriage is twenty-four hours a day and seven days a week. And in that testing-place, there were both grace moments that showed the best sides of him and truth moments that showed the worst sides of him.

Anyone who's married will tell you the temptation to walk away is real when the honeymoon ends and truth shows up at the door.

In Nathan and Nicole's marriage, there were truths such as years of suppressed anger, unresolved conflict, and poor financial decisions. All of a sudden, Nicole had to choose whether to see her new husband through the lens of grace or the lens of truth. Grace told her to love him, excuse him, and give him time to grow into the man of her dreams. Truth told her to be cautious, remain guarded, and be aware that this could be the man of her nightmares, not her dreams. She decided to listen to both. She graced him by loving him, forgiving him, and giving him room to grow by holding him to the truth that he needed to deal with the man in the private mirror instead of hiding behind the man in the public mirror. She helped him see he couldn't live in public graces while being tormented by private truths. Every day they grew stronger and stronger and closer and closer. Not because they chose the path of grace over truth or truth over grace, but because they chose the path that held them to a marriage of grace *and* truth.

WHEN TRUTH AND GRACE MEET

I'm sure Nicole was afraid of being made a fool of by giving Nathan such grace and truth. She probably replayed the phrase, "Fool me once, shame on you; fool me twice, shame on me" in her mind more than once. Haven't we all been in the same place? Think about every area we've been fooled—relationships, money, business ventures, religious ideals, etc. The list goes on. We feel ashamed, betrayed, and angered when we fall victim to something we think we should have known better than to fall for. No one likes being made a fool of once, let alone twice. So why does it keep happening? Because each one of us *wants* to believe in the principle of second chances. We *want* to believe in the good in people. And we *want* to trust in others more than we want to doubt them. When we give people the benefit of the doubt to change and they don't, we struggle to keep them in good graces with us. We resort to withholding further grace because we have proof that our grace will not be appreciated or valued.

While this makes logical sense to us, it's not the way God works. His philosophy would look something more like this: "Fool Me once, My grace will pick you up; fool Me twice, My truth will keep you up." When we first encounter God's grace, we realize we're picked up, brushed off, and sent off to try again. This reality is often too unbelievable to truly grasp. The result is that we usually end up in the same place, unsure how to live out the grace we've been given. When we encounter God's grace again, we can't help but come face to face with ourselves and realize we need to change some things.

"Fool Me once, My grace will pick you up; fool Me twice, My truth will keep you up."

Admitting we need grace to keep changing us is what makes the truth evident to us.

How we apply and filter grace and truth to ourselves and others is often rooted in our understanding of these two concepts from God. If you don't believe in God, His grace, or His truth, it's difficult to fully understand the magnitude and role of grace and truth in our everyday lives. Trying to fathom the depth and love of a God who is unmoved and undeterred by even the most heinous of offenses, without actually having a relationship with Him, is like a lifelong vegetarian trying to grasp what a filet mignon tastes like. It's not that they're wrong for never tasting steak. They just have no point of reference. God, through Jesus, breaks the known rules of both grace and truth to paint for us a picture that perfectly merges the two to be our point of reference. Scripture tells us in John, *"For the law was given through Moses, but grace and truth came through Jesus Christ"* (John 1:17 NKJV).

Grace alone didn't just come through Jesus and truth by itself didn't just come through Jesus. Both grace and truth came through Him.

But *why?* Why did God send both to us?

Because truth was too hard to live up to, God had to break His own rules to give us a bridge back into relationship with Him—in other words, Jesus. He sees our need to be birthed in truth while formed in grace. No matter how much we try to live in truth, we'll all miss the mark at some point. Even the most stellar of employees will one day lose a customer. Even the most obedient of children will fail at something sooner or later. And even the most faithful spouse will let you down once in a while. We can only do our best with truth before we need grace to step in.

When we admit our truth is flawed or incomplete, we open ourselves up to the possibility that every truth we hold to is wrong. And when we admit our perspective on grace is skewed, we're forced to accept that the life we're currently living may not be all that God has for us. Breaking either set of rules is a risk, but holding on to rules that keep you living a marginal life is an even greater risk. God doesn't want you to get to the end and realize you've spent your entire life with the wrong image of Him. He wants you to start to know Him differently *today* by allowing Him to redefine the vital role His grace and truth play in your life.

Let God break the rules of truth that have caused you to live cautiously and guardedly with Him. Let God change the rules for you through grace to help you make the journey back to His truth. And let Him show you that everything you've been missing in your life can be found in both truth and grace.

Too many of those who know God personally still live from limited truth about His unlimited grace because they stay hostage to who they've been. They feel like there are only so many spots on their punch card of grace, so they don't live out of the freedom of favor. They live in this battle trying to understand what God will and will not grace, trying not to use up all their grace punches on the small sins, thinking, *I'll live with the guilt of the small stuff and let grace handle the big stuff.*

The problem with this mentality is that even the small stuff adds up to big stuff and eventually you'll run out of grace for both. But God's grace doesn't ever run out. Ever. It carries you out of everything you've done in your past into a future that starts every day with a clean slate. It doesn't ask why you did it, but asks you why you're still letting it define you. It positions you to be next no matter how many times you blow it. It takes the truth of what you've done and begins to weave in an invitation for you to live beyond those past choices. The closer you move to the truth of who God is, the closer you come to accepting His grace for who you are.

No matter how hard we try to grasp, explain, and define grace and truth, the reality is only God can reveal them to us. This book doesn't claim to have all the answers about this enormous, grandiose God we're endeavoring to know. Its intention is to simply start you on a journey of relationship where He finds you right where you are to start a conversation that will eventually lead you to where you need to be. Fill up the sides of these pages with the quiet revelations God speaks to you as you read each chapter. Keep a record of all the questions, thoughts, ideas, and even emotions you have as He leads you toward a greater understanding of Him and yourself.

And don't keep this journey with God to yourself. The marriage of truth and grace isn't just needed for the Christian or for the church. This cohesive model is needed in our homes, our workplaces, and our communities. Share it with others who are trying to understand this God who doesn't seem to fit into their world. Help them see that if God cares so much about you He'd write a book about breaking your rules, then He must want to do the same in their life as well. Maybe, just maybe, if He can change the way we understand and experience Him, His grace, and His truth, then He will change the way the world sees Him, too.

The least likely are the most likely.

3

QUALIFYING THE UNQUALIFIED

"What qualifies you is your willingness to go forward unqualified."
—Anonymous

Have you ever started a job and thought, *How did I get hired—I am so not qualified!* Or received a promotion seemingly without cause, or found yourself in a relationship with someone who's "out of your league"?

Position can either set you up to feel like you're a success or set you up to feel like a failure. Ask the oldest kid in a family, and they'll tell you the pros and cons for being first. Talk to any football player, and they'll give you an earful about the ins and outs of the best field position. Talk to any brand analyst, and they'll have a strong opinion on the proper product positioning. No two positions are the same, and no two positions carry the same weight of responsibility. When we believe we're positioned correctly, we naturally gravitate toward success and accolades. When we believe we're positioned poorly, we instinctively move away from the limelight to hide in mediocrity.

Each positon we play at work, at home, at school, on the field, at church, or anywhere else will eventually lead us to an internal *disposition*.

Unfortunately, even when our outward positions change, our inward dispositions can be slow to react. How we transition into new positions is directly linked to our inward position on whether we believe we are actually qualified to make that transition. In other words, new positions may present themselves to us, but our inward position dictates our decisions to either step in or step out of these new positions. For example, if a new mom and dad feel they are qualified to be new parents, they'll embrace the role whole-heartedly. But if they feel they are too inexperienced or incapable, they'll instinctively pull back and constantly second-guess themselves. Their new position of responsibility will be trumped by their inward disposition of fear and insecurity.

This internal battle is what I call a *faith gap*.

Faith gaps occur when we struggle inwardly to accept we are qualified for things that at one time were out of our reach. This break of faith begins when our *inward disposition* stands opposite our *outward position*. It's the tug of war between who we are and who we believe, think, and say we are.

What forms our inward disposition? Well, most of us look to our past and then at our present to determine what we are and aren't qualified for. Each of these glances behind and around us serves as a mental scorecard as we rate our qualifications for what we should pursue or avoid in life. If you scored poorly in a writing class in high school, you likely would count yourself unqualified to write a book. If you scored badly in a marriage that ended in divorce, you would most likely deem yourself unfit to live happily ever after. If you haven't been first in line for promotions, you won't apply for that open managerial position.

Once you've heard enough times that you're unqualified, you might begin to think you're unqualified for almost everything. It creeps into your everyday life and vocabulary until you have no desire to ever show up to another opportunity just to hear you're not the one.

If you tolerate your faith gaps, they eventually, quietly, become dominant beliefs that lead you to sabotage what God has already qualified you to accomplish. They become the silent assassins of our advancement. Opportunity may come knocking, but if we don't inwardly believe we're qualified, we'll never answer the door.

THE UNLIKELY KING

As the youngest of eight sons, David understood what it was like to not be "the one." His position as the youngest boy in the family seemed a precursor to what his position would be for the rest of his life—last in line. No one looked at him to be the answer, the solution, or the hero.

David wasn't qualified. Period.

Opportunity may come knocking, but if we don't inwardly believe we're qualified, we'll never answer the door.

So when God sent Samuel the prophet to David's father's house to anoint a new king, David didn't even show up. (See 1 Samuel 16.) While all seven of his brothers went through the purification process to be considered a possibility for kingship, David stayed out in the field among the filth, the animals, and the drudgery. He must have thought, *For sure it can't be me.* He convinced himself that the proper position for him was out on the field, not next to his brothers, his father, or his home. He took the only position he felt he was qualified to take—a shepherd boy, not a son.

How many times have we taken the same position as David because we didn't feel qualified, eligible, or adequate? How many times have we chosen to not even show up because we already knew we wouldn't be chosen? How many times have we predetermined that we will never be the answer, the solution, or the hero? How many conversations have we sat through in silence because we felt speaking our ideas would be above our position? It's easy to see how the *feeling* of being unqualified can lead us to actually *believe* we're unqualified.

But what happens when God wants to break the rules to use the unqualified instead of the qualified? What happens when the one person you'd least expect to be king is actually the one God wants? What happens when God passes over all the expected candidates in the right positions to choose instead the unexpected one who isn't qualified?

Unlikely events, that's what happens. At least that's what happened to David.

All seven of David's brothers stood in line in anticipation, and one by one the prophet Samuel says, "This one is not the one God has chosen." Finally, Samuel asks if there are any other sons left. David's rugged, dirty face out in the field must have flashed through all of their minds. *The prophet can't be talking about* David, *can he?* they all thought. It just didn't seem possible that the one God wanted would be the youngest son, the forgotten one.

Can you imagine being the firstborn and hearing your position doesn't automatically qualify you? Or being the handsomest, and hearing it's not you? Or the tallest? Or the strongest? Or the smartest? What a paradoxical position for these young men. God didn't look to the purification process to qualify David, because David didn't go through the process! God didn't look at the family position for David's credentials, because David was lowest on the totem pole! God didn't take a vote from the brothers to see which one they thought to be worthy, because none of them would have nominated David!

So why David?

God qualified David based on what has always been and will always be invisible to human eyes. God saw what no one else saw in David. *He saw a heart that honored God.*

This scenario gives a renewed sense of hope to us all. For everyone who feels success is impossible because they were born in the wrong neighborhood, born with the wrong last name, or born into a family in the wrong social position, David's life is a constant reminder that the unqualified can become the qualified. For everyone who feels they've made too many mistakes or missed the mark too many times, this story champions hope that God sees us and isn't done with us yet.

When we read stories like this, we desperately want to understand why God chooses the least likely. We'd much prefer a simple three steps to success. We want to put God in a box so that we can understand how He works, but there is simply no quantifiable logic to comprehend the method of God's qualifications. God defies logic. He doesn't look at us like we look at one another. He doesn't pursue the qualified to accomplish His plans and purposes, but instead chooses to look deep into the things only He can see. Jesus, on behalf of the Father, searches the inward intentions, thoughts, and motives of the unqualified to bridge a genuine relationship with each of us, regardless of our outward qualifications. The lowliest to the greatest now stand before God, equal and acceptable in His sight because of His Son.

God defies logic. He doesn't look at us like we look at one another.

This cracks wide open the characteristics of the kind of people God can use. No longer are only the prestigious allowed to be positioned for greatness. God breaks through rules to find those that may not qualify socially, but do qualify spiritually. His freedom from the stifling man-made measuring sticks that plague our society offers the same refuge and peace to the sinner as to the righteous, to the unbeliever as to the believer, to the disadvantaged as to the advantaged. A genuine and humanly-flawed relationship with Him becomes the great equalizer for everyone. We can all come equally before the only One who can break every rule to expose in us what He calls *worthy*.

FROM PORN STAR TO BELOVED DAUGHTER

Brittni wasn't someone you'd expect God to break the rules for. Growing up, rejection and heartbreak was all she ever knew, and she longed for a true love that would make her feel like the princess she fantasized of becoming. But as young as sixteen, her quest for the attention and approval she lacked at home led her to strip onstage at a club in Mexico. The beginning seeds of lust-disguised-as- love were planted in her heart that night as men threw attention, money, and unbridled desire at her. For the first time in her life, Brittni felt beautiful, wanted, and loved. Two years later, while Brittni attended college in hopes of becoming a broadcast journalist, she once again found herself stripping to earn money. It was the one job she thought she was qualified for. The applause, the admiration, and the adoration began to fulfill a part of her heart that had never felt good enough before.

One night after stripping, she was approached with an offer to start doing pornography. She took it. Unaware of the possible consequences, Brittni saw it only as an opportunity to make more money, finish school, and ultimately find the life she had been hoping for. No one looked beyond the surface to see a hurting and broken young woman on the road to self-destruction. At just eighteen, Brittni found herself lost in an industry that seemed to disqualify her from everything she had once dreamed of as a young girl.

After her first porn movie, Brittni quickly rose to fame and began a career in the adult entertainment industry that seemed to offer unlimited success, promotion, and accomplishment as the awards and accolades rolled in. For seven years, she reigned as one of the most esteemed and acclaimed porn stars. But when the cameras were turned off and the paychecks were spent, Brittni knew her life was out of control. She went on to film over three hundred adult movies and, with each recording, she fell deeper and deeper into an abyss of shame and guilt. She was engulfed in a daily cycle of depression, drugs, and sex. Gone was the promise of a legitimate career. Gone was the dream of ever being carried off by Prince Charming. Gone was the belief that she could ever be anything more than a slave to an industry that used and abused her.

Chained to a life of violent relationships, sexual diseases, and demeaning sex, Brittni found herself without hope. What began as a way to fill her insecurity and rejection was spiraling into a gaping hole of pain as she saw herself as worthy of being nothing more than a sex slave. Broken by the manipulation and control of the industry, Brittni felt the only position she was qualified for was the one given to her by directors and producers. Misery overshadowed the glitz and glamour that the public saw. The pain

Brittni secretly lived with was hidden behind a stage name that had quickly lost its luster.

Throughout the years, Brittni had never been against church but stayed at bay simply because she didn't believe she was welcome. Her sins seemed to disqualify her from even walking through the doors. But as she sank deeper into the darkness of porn, she became more and more desperate to get out. At the invitation of her grandfather, Brittni decided to try church. It was there that she met the one Man who loved the real Brittni despite all her shame, guilt, addictions, and pain. It was as though, for the first time in her life, someone had turned the light on all the secret sins of her soul, the darkest parts of her heart, and the deepest pains of her life. But instead of condemning her or turning away from her, Jesus leaned in close and wrapped her in His arms of unconditional love.

After accepting Jesus as her Savior, Brittni began a long journey back to freedom. One layer at a time, Jesus began to delve behind the façade of the porn star to reveal a young woman who still desperately wanted to be loved. Deep in her heart, she questioned how God could wipe away her past and give her a brand new start. Didn't He see how dirty and stained she had become? Didn't He see the only real job qualification she had was sex? Didn't He see the long list of sins that disqualified her from being anything noble, remarkable, and extraordinary? Didn't He see all the rules that stood in the way of her being truly saved?

As she read His Word, as she learned to have a relationship with Him personally, and as she began to believe in His voice more than any other, God began to break rules to position her, not for judgment and pain, but for His plans and purposes.

The breakthrough moment for her was when she was invited to our Uprising Young Adult service and heard a man preach a message that forever changed her life. Though he didn't know he was speaking directly to her, his words cut through her low self-esteem and brokenness to reveal the woman on the inside who was worth the wait. For the first time in her entire life, Brittni heard and believed that she was a woman of God and worth the wait of true love. His message radically changed how she saw herself and her worth and led her to take a vow of singleness for one year to learn how to pursue purity and wait for the man who was willing to wait for her.

That man who was willing to wait for her turned out to the same man that spoke to her at our church. My nephew, Richard, watched this young woman fall more in love with God every day, and he couldn't help but fall more in love with her as well. In 2016, I had the honor of marrying this incredible couple and watching Brittni walk down the altar in a beautiful white gown, gleaming with genuine beauty and grace. They now speak to thousands around the world about the truth behind the porn industry, the truth of Jesus, and the truth about real love that will wait. On a weekly basis God qualifies Brittni to be His spokesperson to the world and positions her to live in the dreams she once held as a small child. Not only did she meet the Prince Charming she thought didn't exist, but now together they are raising a generation of young people who are passionately pursuing purity.

To God, Brittni isn't a porn star who got saved.
She's a daughter who has come home
to tell the world about the God who
broke the rules to find her.

Today, if you met Brittni, you would meet a young woman who bears no resemblance to the stage name that was her identity for almost a decade. The platform she gained through the porn industry pales in comparison to the stage God is now giving her and Richard. This young couple serves as a brazen billboard of God's illogical favor, blessing, and forgiveness.

By all accounts, Brittni and Richard shouldn't be leading a thriving ministry at our church, but they are. They shouldn't be positioned as ambassadors around the world for God's grace, but they are. They shouldn't be asked to do interviews on radio stations and television stations around the nation, but they are.

Why would God use *Brittni* when she's had more years in the adult entertainment industry than in the church?

People criticized my wife and me for allowing Brittni to be vocal about her story in our church. In their perspective, her transformation needed to be handled with caution and discretion. I disagreed then and still do today. If God had qualified her at the altar to be His daughter, then she is qualified to share her journey with anyone who will listen. To God, Brittni isn't a porn star who got saved. She's a daughter who has come home to tell the world about the God who broke the rules to find her.

WHEN THE UNQUALIFIED BECOME THE QUALIFIED

Maybe your story isn't like Brittni's on the outside. Maybe you didn't run to the porn industry to find your identity. Maybe you didn't showcase your sins publicly like she did. But, at one time or another, we've all felt like we have disqualified ourselves. We've all felt like there is no way God could use us because of the myriad of poor decisions we made that led us down a road we didn't expect. The sin you're living in may not be sexual, but shame and guilt are still familiar friends you've learned to live with. The industry you're hiding in may be business, education, or even ministry, but God still sees you.

God still wants you.

At some point in your life you're going to run into an area where your finances, your achievements, your accolades, and your personal successes are not going to be enough to cut it. Think of some of the great icons of our day that seem to be synonymous with success—Michael Jordan, Steve Jobs, Steven Spielberg, Oprah Winfrey, and Walt Disney. You may think the only thread that links these famous names together is prominence and success, but you'd be wrong. They also each share a tale of defeat, failure, and rejection. At some point in the early days of their careers, they all found themselves disqualified and dejected. Today, their early stories may reflect your life more accurately than their later success. You may be just starting a new business venture and can't seem to get it funded. You might be starting a career in a field among company bosses who keep passing you by, promotion after promotion.

You may even be a college graduate with a bachelor's or master's degree and still be unemployed. More and more, young people are looking to the generations before them to help them find the tools and resources they need to qualify for a life of genuine significance. In universities across America, there seems to be a philosophical war raging over this question: is the primary purpose of higher education to teach for knowledge and personal insight or to train graduates for the job market? There are proponents on either side, but students are the only real victims. The lack of clear agreement results in thousands of millennials feeling frustrated and unqualified to acquire and maintain a successful career like they saw their parents achieve. Those same millennials who are struggling now to be qualified through experience and education will eventually be in power positions as they outnumber every other generation before them.

If *we* can't answer the question on how to best qualify them for their future, we need to make sure we introduce them to the God who does.

There has never been a more pertinent time than now to believe in *who* qualifies us more than *what* qualifies us. With the constant pressure to perform in the boardroom, the classroom, and the salesroom, it's virtually impossible to qualify in every area of our lives. Perhaps you qualify morally, but you're missing professionally. Or maybe you trump your peers intellectually, but you're not polished socially. Or maybe your portfolio is stocked creatively, but lacking academically. Or maybe you're well-regarded ministerially, but you're not astute relationally. Whatever your strengths and weakness are, we all tip the scales of qualified and unqualified at one point or another. Our goal must not be to find recognition in either our success or our failures, but rather to let our identity recognize both, and then move on to be defined by Christ instead. Often God waits until we're ready to accept both our personal highs and our personal lows to position us in the most unlikely of places.

DOUBTS DON'T DISQUALIFY

Why would God want to favor the ones others only criticize? And why would He want to break the rules of position to promote the ones others would never choose? Why David? Why Brittni?

Because when God does the unthinkable with a person, their life becomes an illogical paradox that the world wants to understand. For every redemptive story like Brittni's or yours, there are hundreds of people who want to know *why*. That search to understand a God who doesn't make sense leads to an encounter with the God they themselves need as well.

When God does the unthinkable with a person, their life becomes an illogical paradox that the world wants to understand.

In his early days, the apostle Paul had some real arguments with Jesus and those who followed Him. He questioned Jesus' identity as the Messiah and refused to accept the teachings of His disciples. He had serious issues connecting the dots between the God he knew in Scripture and the God who came to earth as the Savior of the world. His arguments led him on a mission that seemed counterproductive to his religious beliefs. He was a devoutly religious man, yet he was also a murderer. And by the nature of his barbaric ways, you'd assume he would be the *least* likely to one day be a Jesus-follower like those he hated. But his murdering mission led him to the truth. (See Acts 9.) His questions and doubt brought him face-to-face with a God he could no longer deny. In essence, you could say his hatred for Jesus led him to experience the illogical love of Jesus.

For the doubter and critic in all of us, I would hope we all find ourselves in the same position Paul found himself. Not disqualified because of his own doubts, but qualified because of God's unwavering grace.

I once knew a brilliant university researcher and teacher of evolutionary science who struggled to connect the dots between creation and evolution. Though he was more than qualified scientifically on the subject of creation, he couldn't shake his ignorance theologically. His faith carried one idea but his knowledge of science seemed to offer a different one. He decided to do something completely unorthodox with the creation account in Genesis.

With meticulous detail, he researched the biblical story of creation from the perspective of a scientific theory and discovered more than he bargained for. Not only was he able to scientifically give evidence that validated both science and Scripture, his journey led him to know the Creator more authentically.

You may not be interested in arguing creation versus evolution, but there are questions in all of us about the parts of God that just don't make sense to us. You might be struggling to connect the dots between success and significance, faith and logic, or calling and vocation. Whatever questions you have, your quest for truth doesn't disqualify you from knowing the Truth-Teller. Too many people are fearful of questioning God about the things that don't make sense to them, and they end up isolated from the One who wants to give them the answers to their deepest inquisitions. Every *why* you wrestle with internally is intended to push you toward the *Who* that embraces your humanity. If we would let go of the notion that our arguments, questions, and hesitations with God somehow disqualify us, we would begin to see that He uses our very disagreements to draw us closer to Him.

IT'S NOT UP TO YOU ANYMORE

Look at your life and think of every reason you feel disqualified. Take a minute and come up with all the reasons why you believe you're not the one for that job, that relationship, or that award. Grab a piece of paper and write down every fact that you see as evidence why you shouldn't be asked to sit at the table of greatness at work, at school, at home, or with peers. Don't leave out one excuse. Make it long. Include every argument you have with a future marked by influence, affluence, and prestige. And when you've articulated every doubt, every question, and every excuse, throw the list in the trash. Burn it. Shred it. And walk away. You don't need it anymore. You never did. It's the paradox of position that you've wrestled with for too long. It's the struggle for *more* in you that wars against the lie of *less* that has lived in you.

It's time to grab a new sheet of paper and write all the reasons why He's already qualified you. Write down every crazy idea that you've never believed before but always wanted to. Let a new chapter in your life begin, one without excuses, fears, doubts, and arguments.

You don't get to decide whether or not you are qualified.

Now, I know some of you may be laughing at the audacity of change being so easy. I realize the realist in you may be even offended that I'm handing out what some might call "false hope." You look at your life and think that it might work in principle, but never in practice. But isn't this the same simplistic principle we use to accept other aspects in our life? We look at a doctor's list of physical evidence, and we widely accept it to be truth. We look at a list of bills and accept that debt will indefinitely be part of our future. We look at a list of stock trends and base our financial decisions on the hopes of predictions. We look at a weather report and accede to a forecast of educated guesses. We accept the evidence before us and make our life decisions on it. It's not far-fetched, unreasonable, or illogical.

Yet, when God says, "Look at a list of all the reasons I say you're qualified," we struggle to believe it. We argue there isn't sufficient evidence to accept what we can't see. But I ask you, how many people have you known who were misdiagnosed by a doctor? How many times have you played the odds on the stock market and lost? How many times have you carried an umbrella in preparation for a storm that never came? If you can say yes to even one of these questions, I would hope you'd be willing to reconsider the possibility that a new list of God's qualifications based on the past actions of this all-powerful God might be just enough to start the process of change in all of us. Story after story of people just like Brittni stand as proof of God's paradoxical qualification process. Will you believe in it for your own life?

Our beliefs are the catalyst for change. What we believe, we ultimately attract, whether it be negative or positive. If we believe that closed doors can open for us, we'll move toward the possibility of opportunity. If we believe we *don't* have the right to access opportunity, we'll end up in the position farthest from the door.

If you buy into beliefs that you're not good enough, not educated enough, not privileged enough, then you need to say, "Enough!" If you need a change of position today, start with a change of opinion of God, yourself, and your future. Nothing is out of your reach when God's opinion is part of your speech. Nothing is unattainable when you take the position of teachable. Nothing is unachievable when you change what you believe is conceivable.

Over the years, I've watched the least likely become the most likely more times than I can count. I've watched marriages find their way back to reconciliation when hope was lost. I've watched young people dream and achieve greater things than they thought possible. This I know and this I remember: God doesn't give to one and withhold from another. He is a giver of destiny equally. He favors His creation universally. He graces each of us impartially. He's just waiting for us to believe in Him as much as He believes in us.

Life is not a test you pass or fail. It's not a game you win or lose. It's a journey toward discovery that's filled with lessons learned, skills acquired, and obstacles triumphed over that will one day lead you to understand everything you question today. Nothing in your past can disqualify you from your future unless you let it. Start believing now in the God who has already prequalified you for the life you were meant to live. Give Him a chance to pull out the credentials in you that others have overlooked and criticized. Open your heart and mind again to the possibility of things that you felt you didn't deserve.

You may be out in the field of your life, dirty like David, broken like Brittni, or confused like Paul, but God has already chosen you to be the answer. He's already sent a Someone to look beyond those who seem the logical choice to find you. He's already broken the rules so you would believe in you again and in His incredible plan for your life. All He is waiting for is you.

All you have to lose are the rules God needs to break.

The harder you look for recognition,
the harder it is to find it.

4

NEW RULES OF RECOGNITION

*"Don't worry when you're not recognized,
but strive to be worthy of recognition."*
—Abraham Lincoln

In 1990, one of the world's most expensive paintings sold for $82.5 million, but the artist never saw a cent. He had passed away a century before without a penny to his name. Now one of the most renowned painters in history, when Van Gogh was alive, he was a tormented, twisted soul who knew only failure. In fact, many historians believe Van Gogh sold only one portrait before he committed suicide.

How does an overlooked, mentally ill artist become one of the most famous and influential painters of all time?

Recognition.

After his death, Van Gogh's brother, Theo, began to introduce the world to Vincent's work, but then he, too, died only a few months later. Theo's wife,

Johanna, continued her husband's mission and began to sell, loan, and pub-
lish the unknown masterpieces of Van Gogh to the art world. But she didn't
just showcase his pieces as an artist, she put his private torment on display
as well. She published the letter correspondences between Van Gogh and
his brother. The world fell in love with the story of a madman whose only
momentary solace when he was alive was found in the brushstrokes of the
masterpieces he left behind.

Vincent Van Gogh was the brilliant artist, but Johanna Van Gogh was
the improbable genius who brought his name to the world.

When Jesus was alive He performed many miracles, but it was His final
miraculous act of resurrection that brought infinite recognition to the Son
of God. It was only through His death that we could recognize His true
divinity. And just like Van Gogh, Jesus needed somebody to bring His name
to the world. Actually, He needed twelve somebodies. The disciples were to
Jesus what Johanna was to Van Gogh. They took the message of Jesus and
refused to let it die with His death. They gave their lives to ensure He was
recognized as more than just a teacher, prophet, and man. They were the
unlikely heroes who brought Jesus to the world so that He could be recognized not only by God, but by man as well.

A HUNGER FOR RECOGNITION OR AFFIRMATION?

I realize not everyone is a fan of recognition. Recognition has gotten
a bad rap over the years because it seems to go hand-and-hand with pride,
arrogance, and self-promotion. There seem to be unspoken rules about recognition that paint a picture of God being *against* recognition. But recognition by man is not the same as recognition by God. When man calls you, it's
based on what man sees, but when God calls you, it's based on what He sees.
And even though His vantage point always exceeds that of man, God is not
against recognizing a job well done.

In one parable in the book of Matthew, Jesus tells the story of a master
who entrusted his finances into the hands of his servants. Two of the servants invested the money while the last servant hid his portion in fear.
When the master returned, he openly recognized and praised the two who
wisely invested and managed his money, saying to each, *"Well done, good and*

faithful servant; you were faithful over a few things, I will make you ruler over many things. Enter into the joy of your lord" (Matthew 25:21 NKJV).

This parable is an analogy of the kingdom of heaven with the master's words clearly reflecting God's pleasure in recognizing acts of faithfulness, diligence, and hard work. God isn't against recognition. He actually finds joy in recognizing our commitment to hard work and excellence as His sons and daughters!

In God's eyes, *recognition* isn't a bad word.

The first step to accepting recognition from God is realizing that while man can call you, only God can call you *and* choose you. This single differentiator eradicates every barrier that stands before you and me in our workplaces, schools, ministries, and families. God's recognition calls you, chooses you, and positions you to break free from a life paralyzed by intimidation, inferiority, and inadequacy.

And it's not your merits or faults that determine His call and recognition on your life. God calls and chooses us based on His prewritten plan and our spiritual pursuit for Him rather than the qualifications predetermined by man. This truth dissipates the torment of wondering whether we will be rejected or accepted by man. Because He calls you and chooses you, you can live in *His* recognition instead of hungering after the affirmation of man.

Over the years I've met many people who've had the call of man on their life. Their talent, gifting, and personality made them seem like the obvious choice for promotion and favor. But I've come to realize more and more that the call of man cannot sustain you if the call of God is not within you. On the other hand, when the call of God is in you, even if the call of man shifts to someone with greater talent, greater gifting, or greater personality, you won't be left trying to figure out what to do next. When the temptation comes to seek out the audible validation, approval, and recognition of man, you will still desire the inaudible call of God *more*. The fame, attention, and applause will not be what you seek first. God's call may still include fame, notoriety, and applause, but that won't be the primary focus for your life. It won't be what satisfies you on a deep, personal level.

Ever since I was a teenager, I've felt the call of man. Success came to me early as a semi-professional skateboarder, then a renowned deejay, then an affluent entrepreneur. But the one calling in my life that has surpassed every other is *pastor*. I felt accomplishment when I listened to the call of man—as skateboarder, deejay, entrepreneur. But when I answered the call of God to be a pastor, I began to experience something deeper than accomplishment. I felt *purpose*.

I know you might imagine that I'm talking about being a megachurch pastor on a stage, but I'm not. I'm referring to the call of God to serve people at whatever capacity He chooses for me. Today, I get to see God break the rules for people who don't deserve it, don't understand it, and don't expect it. I've watched banks deny loans and then turn around and change their mind because God stepped in. I've watched marriages on the road to disaster rip up divorce papers because God got involved. I've seen doctor's reports filled with astonishment because God answered a prayer of someone previously diagnosed as ill or dying. God's call is what brings me a deeper sense joy, excitement, passion, and fulfillment. At the end of my life I will know I lived out not only the call of man, but also the call of God.

And you don't have to be a pastor to know the call of God. My parents, the wonderful Salvador and Soledad De La Mora, were not pastors or ministers of any kind, but they knew the call of God. They were immigrants who devoted their entire lives to raising their family, building a prestigious landscape design company, and successfully managing real estate in Santa Barbara. In the perspective of some, their success and their bank account means that they must have lived out the call of man. But my life and the lives of my brothers and sisters are proof they lived out the call of God.

Over the years, both of my parents consistently sacrificed their own personal preferences in order to focus instead on raising a God-fearing family who worked together, dreamed together, fought together, and succeeded together. Their countless prayers and words of wisdom were birthed in the throne room of heaven and lived deep within their hearts. My mother was a loyal wife who tirelessly stood beside my father's dream. They modeled teamwork, sacrificial love, and relentless parenting because they believed it was their mandate from God. In their lives here with us, they desired no recognition, praise, or applause for the simple yet profound existence they lived. They lived in obscurity so their family would be honored publicly for the values, ethics, and morals they had instilled.

When my mom passed away earlier this year, the depth of my parents' legacy was felt in the countless stories that were intertwined with tears of sadness and gratitude from their children, grandchildren, and great-grand-children. For generations to come, the legacy of Salvador and Soledad De La Mora will live on in the recognition, adoration, and praise of the family they raised.

My parents understood that legacy brings a recognition far surpassing public praise or adoration. It's the kind of recognition that lasts a lifetime. The kind of recognition that is passed on from one generation to the next. My parents may have not been looking for recognition in their life, but recognition came looking for them.

FOLLOWING THE CALL OF GOD

The truth is the harder we look for notoriety, the more it evades us. And it's also true that the harder we try to hide in obscurity, the more recognition seeks to invade us. In fact, I've found that it's our desire to work in secret that inclines God to want to show off His work in public. Just because no one else sees the blood, sweat, and tears you've been pouring out in silence at home or at work doesn't mean God didn't see it! All the hours of quiet sacrifice and faithfulness never go unnoticed to God. And while behind-the-scenes may not be the most glorious position in the ladder of success, it's the perfect formula for God to break the rules.

Too many people follow the rules of success in hopes of finding the lime-light and fame that society offers—but end up disappointed. Perhaps it's because God knows so well that the ladder of success doesn't lead to happi-ness that He offers a different way. His unorthodox methods open wide the doors of promotion to people who once felt as though no one saw their labor. And God's plan is as radical as His methods. His plan involves knowing *you* more than knowing your résumé.

Our accolades or failures are often our personal indicator of what we believe we are qualified for. When we shrink back because we see more failures than accomplishments, we leave ourselves out of the running for opportunities. When we step forward and depend only on our past achievements, we are leaning on our own strength and abilities. But God calls us to more. Regardless of our past successes or failures, if we give Him permission to work, God calls us to a greater life than we can imagine. He longs to attach His résumé to ours and position us for much more than we thought feasible.

Your *disbelief in Him* doesn't negate *His belief in you.*

For some of you, this God I'm describing isn't the God you know. Maybe you have never believed in a God who believes this deeply in you. Maybe you've never known God to be personally involved in your successes or failures other than for judgment or punishment. Maybe you've never felt like God sees you.

The good news is your *disbelief in Him* doesn't negate *His belief in you.*

The rules you've carried about who can or can't be promoted shift and change when you begin to accept His rules of promotion. His rules aren't based on what you can or cannot do or what you have or have not done. They're based on what He did already. And even if you've never known Him before, today is a good day to start. You've got nothing to lose but all the rules and regulations that limited who you can be.

God is calling you to more!

FINDING IDENTITY AGAIN

I realize it's a risk to respond to God's call and beckoning if you have never heard it or haven't heard it in a while, but remember that despite the risk, what awaits you is far better than what's behind you. David must have known the risks of coming to the table when he was called in from the field. He must have known that all his other brothers had gone through the purification process before standing in front of the prophet Samuel. He must have known that no one wanted him at the table, or they would have called for him sooner.

I'm sure some crazy questions were running through his head on the way to the house from the field. *Why am I being called? If I've never been called before, why do they want me now? Is this a joke?* My guess would be that never in his wildest dreams did he imagine he was about to be called king. Can you imagine the humiliation David risked by rushing in from the field covered in dirt and manure and seeing everyone seated at the table waiting for him? Then to hear that he is being anointed king of Israel? It would be like a college grad being invited to the White House by the president—to take over running the country. Or the janitor being called into the board-room by the CEO—to be his right hand.

If you think this kind of recognition is for fairy tales and Bible stories, then you haven't met Dominic.

As a kid, Dominic seemed destined for greatness. Brilliant with a knack for numbers and getting along with people, his peers, teachers, and parents saw him as the natural-born leader and looked to him to be the one to set the example. When it came time for him to submit applications to college, acceptance seemed inevitable. Within a few months, his acceptance letter came and Dominic seemed a shoo-in for a corporate career, a corner office, and a six-figure salary. But Dominic never made it to graduation. After two years away from home at college, the pressure began to eat away at him. He was lost and unsure of himself but didn't think he could turn to anyone for help. Quickly his anxiety turned into depression and he began to withdraw from everyone he knew. Those who knew him best couldn't understand the shift from the young man who at one time was confident, happy, and des-tined for success but now was apathetic and withdrawn. He dropped out, and drifted.

Less than five years later, Dominic was homeless and working as a jani-tor at an accounting firm. He walked with his head down and spoke to only a handful of people, but he ached to be part of the conversations he heard around him as he swept the floors of the corporate offices. He longed to wear a freshly pressed suit like the men and women he cleaned up after. He desperately wanted to be connected to a world he was obviously unqualified for. Yet he dreamed anyway. Arriving before anyone else and staying long past everyone left, Dominic imagined what it would be like to come in not as the help but as a colleague.

I met Dominic at a Meet and Greet at one of our campuses and was surprised at the eloquence and intelligence of the haggard young man in front of me. He spoke with a quiet acumen that carried both graceful wisdom and raw experience. After spending a few minutes together, he looked at me with eyes that had seen more than most people twice his age, and said, "Pastor, I don't think God is pleased with my life. I think I'm living the wrong life." The hunger in Dominic's face as he said that rivaled any man with diplomas on his wall and money in the bank.

He went on to tell me that though he had done all the wrong things in his life and walked away from the path that seemed to be laid out for him at an early age, he'd still held on to a relationship with God. He kept praying and carried around a weathered, aged Bible, but he had never felt that God was genuinely pleased with him. He said he went to church every week because he knew it was what he was supposed to do even though he didn't feel worthy of going. I listened quietly and, when he was done, asked him just one question: "Dominic, do you believe that God called you to be a janitor?" He paused for a long time, put his head down, and said quietly, "I don't think so."

"Dom," I said, "Just because you're reading His Word and coming to church doesn't mean you're living out your call. God is calling you to more."

Over the next few months, Dominic began to ask himself the harder questions. What was he really created for and purposed to do in life? What really brought him a sense of joy and happiness? What would he be doing if he hadn't made the choices he'd made as a young student? Slowly, Dominic began to realize he still loved numbers and people, and that his job as a janitor at an accounting firm was a second chance at both. He decided to take a few steps out of his shell and take every conversation around him as an opportunity to learn. He watched and listened and began to understand more than anyone thought a janitor would know.

During his lunch, he'd sit and engage any of the accountants who would give him the chance to pick their brain. To them, Dominic was amusing. To Dominic, they were mentors. Soon he was able to keep up with their conversations.

One day, while he was mopping on the twenty-seventh floor, one of the accountants interrupted his work and asked Dominic to follow him. Walking into the boardroom in his raggedy uniform, Dominic stood embarrassed in front of the panel of men in pristine suits. The company, the panel explained, was starting a partnership program with a local college that would allow students to gain experience and employment through their company. Dominic was asked to be their first student employee. Speechless, Dominic tried to explain that he wasn't even in college, but the panel wasn't interested. The CEO extended his hand and Dominic reached out and shook it.

You see, as Dominic cleaned toilets, swept floors, and took out trash, God was preparing him for much more. Dominic just needed to let God break the rules.

SOME RULES ARE MEANT TO BE BROKEN

How many of us have looked to our own life and wondered the same thing as Dominic? How many times have we showed up to work on the outside without really showing up on the inside? Have we ever operated halfheartedly at home, at school, or at work because we didn't get the recognition we felt we deserved?

Recent studies by Gallup tell us that more than half of employees are unengaged or actively disengaged at work.[1] Could it be that the majority of our workforce has lost the heart to follow their passion and instead go after a stable paycheck regardless of whether it makes them miserable or joyful? Do we still have a pursuit to follow after the call of God? To receive man's recognition, you will have to abide by man's rules. And man's recognition might lead you to *success*, but it will never lead you to *satisfaction*. Satisfaction comes only from being recognized by God.

---

1. See Amy Adkins, "Majority of U.S. Employees Not Engaged," Gallup.com, January 28, 2015, http://www.gallup.com/poll/181289/majority-employees-not-engaged-despite-gains-2014.aspx (accessed May 15, 2017).

Here's the beauty of it: God's recognition of you gives you the permission to break the rules in your life that need to be broken so that you can live the life you were meant to live.

Every rule that confined you is actually intended to liberate you. It's only when you allow rules to *define* you that you miss the purpose behind rules. Without rules to stop you, you would never learn how to overcome obstacles. Without rules, you'd never have found the courage and strength to find new methods. Without rules, you would never have stumbled onto the real you. God uses the rules of man to draw us to Him and His true plan for our lives. If you stop too soon, you'll never experience the life lesson hidden in a rule broken. Many people aren't willing to go through this process because it's easier to hide behind the approval or disapproval of man than believe and hope for the approval of God. Like Dominic, if we can believe and begin to walk out a new set of rules for success and recognition, we will see what some would call fairy tales become our reality. Like Dominic, we all want to know a different ending is possible to the story we're currently living. We want to know we're not just stumbling around without a light at the end of the tunnel. The truth is, we all need the recognition of God and man to walk out a new set of rules for success.

Every rule that confined you is actually intended to liberate you.

Think about a young child or teenager you discipline with rules. *Don't touch a hot stove. Don't stay out past curfew. Don't talk to strangers.* While these rules are appropriate for a time, we don't actually expect our children to adhere to them past a certain age. We don't expect our adult children to never touch a hot stove, stay out late, or talk to strangers. They've outgrown those rules. It's not that they weren't needed in their younger years; they've simply outgrown them.

It's the same way for us with God. The problem is that sometimes even as we mature as Christians, we are still holding on to rules that we've outgrown. It's time to let go of some of the rules that still hold you hostage today.

Not every rule was meant to be broken, but not every rule was meant to remain.

If you find yourself running into a wall over and over again in an area of your life, it's a great indicator of an area that needs a new set of rules. If you just can't seem to get through to your spouse and children, you might need some new communication rules for your home. If you are sitting at your desk day after day without life or purpose, you might need a new model for success. If you are struggling to help your church reach the next generation, it's a perfect chance to try out new rules of engagement.

Choosing to live a life drawn out by God's rulebook instead of man's brings a recognition that resonates far deeper than any tangible award or honor. God's recognition of a life marked by His calling is richer, wider, and deeper than we can comprehend. His daily voice will encourage you even during the bleakest of days. His constant presence will guide you when you're not sure which direction to turn. His path of favor will align you when you waver between *the old rules you've known and the new rules you're learning.*

WHEN YOU'RE CHOSEN BY GOD, NOT JUST CALLED BY MAN

I know this for certain: my own aspirations pale in comparison to what God has written for me. All that I attempted to accomplish on my own has never come close to what God has allowed me to be part of since I handed over the rules of my life to Him. No recognition from man has ever compared to hearing and knowing that God is pleased with my life. It is for these reasons that I trust God's voice, even if that means I have to break some rules to obey Him.

What rules is God asking you to let Him break to experience the breakthrough He has waiting for you? Are you holding on to inner rules or vows that say things like: "I will never forgive them"; "I will never do that again"; "I will never hope for this again"; or "I will never let this go"? If you can recognize what needs to be broken, He can do the work for you. And even if you can't right now, will you let Him start the conversation with you? Today your life is the sum result of both the rules you've needed and the rules you've needed to outgrow. Once you begin to open your eyes to the fact that God isn't confined to the rules of man, you might be surprised to see how many archaic rules you've outgrown in your new season of life.

Whether you feel like David in the field who didn't even show up for the possibility of promotion or like Dominic who had seemingly missed his chance at promotion, you are not out of God's sight or off His radar. He's been waiting for the right moment to step in and call you from obscurity. Now is that moment. Your eyes and ears are open to the possibility of things that you were once closed off to and now He can begin to whisper the things He's wanted to deposit into your heart.

The entire reason God challenged me for years to write this book was *you*.

If you didn't grow up in a home that openly recognized your achievements, it may be difficult to believe God would want to recognize you. You won't lean in with an expectation to hear His praise. You won't allow yourself the right to enter into the joy of pleasing Him. You won't live to hear His words of appreciation and acknowledgement. God wants to recognize you, but you've got to let Him break the rules you've held about Him that prevents you from believing He is willing and able to recognize and celebrate you for a job well done.

Whether you've been recognized by man or not, you can now experience the voice of recognition of the One who is unlike any other. His recognition is not on accident or by mistake. It's not because of what you've done or haven't done. It doesn't waver or change. God calls you because He had every intention of calling you before you even took your first breath. He was convinced you were the answer before you opened your eyes or spoke your first word. He placed His DNA inside of you to create a life so vast, so impressive, and so remarkable that it could never be limited to rules. He determined long before the earth was formed that you were the one He would call.

As incredible as this may seem to you, it's true!

In fact, I would go so far as to say the entire reason God challenged me for years to write this book was *you*.

When I didn't think anyone would believe in a God who breaks the rules, He saw you. He saw the faith you would have at this moment to believe that you are called for more, called for greatness, and called by God. He knew that for every second you spent being overlooked, He would give you back more minutes of recognition than you could imagine—recognition from Him and recognition from others. He knew that for every place you'd feel disqualified, He would add His own qualifications to your résumé and give you more opportunity than you could have ever dreamed. Why would He do that for you? For the same reason He did it for me, for David, and for Dominic. If He can convince you that He's the God who breaks the rules to call you, He can use you to convince the people around you.

What does it look like to be recognized by God and not just man?

When you live a life that is marked by the call of God, you will approach each day with a sense of purpose and determination that isn't defined by the rules of success as you understand them today. When you live a life marked by the call of God, you will go to bed every night knowing that we've done all that you could have done to accomplish all that He desires from you. Whether it's in the business, medical, educational, ministerial, parental, or any other field, you'll use every gift, talent, and ability you have to make a difference. You'll enjoy every moment because you recognize every moment as an opportunity to grow, learn, and move toward His dream for you. And you'll live knowing that you weren't just created to live out a *career*, you were born to live out a *call*.

Scarlet is whiter than snow.

5

THE GIFT OF REJECTION

*"Humanity is an ocean; if a few drops of the ocean are dirty,
the ocean does not become dirty."*
—Gandhi

When I was a kid, one of my favorite books was *Harry the Dirty Dog*. A rambunctious white dog with black spots named Harry runs away from his owners to avoid what he hates most—taking a bath—and enjoys a day of pure freedom. He is in dog heaven as he dashes all over the city without a leash through parks, puddles, and construction sites. But at the end of the day, he's become so dirty that he is now a *black* dog with *white* spots. When he makes his way back home, he's so discolored that his family doesn't even recognize him! Desperate to prove his identity, Harry runs upstairs to the bathtub and begs for what he hates. Confident this is not *their* bath-hating dog, but pitying the dog they think is a stray, the family proceeds to bathe Harry. Once his owners begin to wash away evidence of his escapade, they joyfully realize this soiled animal is their beloved family dog. Like every happy ending, Harry is loved and cared for by his family and restored back to a white dog with black spots.

Maybe it was the pastor in me even as a kid, but that story spoke to a core belief I had that no matter how dirty I got in life, I could always come home. It wasn't until many years later that I realized this truth wasn't everyone's story.

THE STORY RULES DON'T TELL

On the outside, Brian was handsome, approachable, and put-together. But Brian's eyes told a different story. He carried the undeniable lines of regret, pain, and shame that couldn't be hidden behind a smile. For over ten years, Brian had struggled with a secret life of homosexuality. He lived with quiet fantasies and buried secrets while wrestling with inward demons he had no idea how to silence. He had been in several relationships but none could squelch the waves of confusion and doubt that surrounded him. He desperately wanted to understand himself and find peace for the raging torment that he lived with every day. He was angry at God, angry at the church, and angry at who he believed he was since birth. He had been raised in a religious home but struggled to find his identity as a young teenager. Searching for significance, he leaned on the people who welcomed him with open arms but soon found himself in friendships that lured him further and further away from God. Surrounded by conflicting voices, Brian felt dirty and stained no matter where he went. He couldn't go home to parents and family who no longer recognized him. He couldn't go back to friends who wanted nothing to do with his search for God. He was too stained to go after God and too clean to keep living a lie. After a decade of trying to find answers to his life, he had come to the end of the rope. So he walked through the doors of our church.

Most people didn't understand why he would choose to attend a church that opposed a life he embraced, but Brian was looking for answers. He was vehemently trying to understand how the God he knew as a small boy could create him and then hate him. He had questions for God that could no longer go unanswered:

Was he too stained to come back to God?

Would God even want him anymore?

Would he ever be able to wash away the stains of a life he wasn't sure he still wanted to embrace?

Would he be able to live out the new creation God had called him to be without the old stains from his past seeping through?

He wrestled with God over and over again and eventually came full circle in his relationship with Him. Brian's stains from his former life were the very reasons he felt combative and angry at God, but each time Brian lashed out, God lovingly reminded him that his stained life was not enough to push Him away. What the world and the church couldn't wash away with rules and stigmas, God cleansed and sanctified with His love.

Brian started with rules that were broken by him and ended with rules that were broken by God. Somewhere in the middle of all the rules being broken for all the wrong reasons, God showed up to tell Brian He saw the man behind those rules.

Brian's story is like countless others' who find themselves unsure of who they are and who they were meant to be. They feel too stained with pain from their choices to go back to the life they chose and too stained with guilt and shame to go forward into change.

Sometimes it takes this conundrum of pain to get us to a place where we're ready to hear truth call our name. Sometimes it takes this fight to discover our real identity that pushes us toward the things we've run from. Sometimes it takes this overwhelming desire to break out of a life you never intended to live to move you forward instead of back. God always seems to show up right when we've got nowhere else to go and nowhere else to turn. Just like Harry the dirty dog, even when our family and friends can't recognize us, God never fails to know us—the real us. He doesn't stand at the door with accusations of where we've been or what we've done. He waits with the water running so He can remind us we're not black with white spots of goodness—we're white from His grace with black spots of human-ity. He lovingly welcomes us back home and washes away every trace of dirt from our adventures without Him. Even if that washing process is one we've hated and run from in the past, God's love and grace draw us back to Him over and over again.

The rules we break and the rules we adhere to show the world who we are in a quick snapshot—good or bad, obedient or defiant, respectful or rebellious, dirty or clean. But what rules *don't* tell are the stories and faces behind each act of obedience or offense. Like Brian, we are more than a list of dos and don'ts or rights and wrongs. We are people in desperate need of a Savior who isn't afraid of diving into our filthy, dirty lives to rescue and redeem us by His sacrifice and love.

That's the beautiful part about the God who breaks the rules. He is the God who sees our hurts, aches, and scars—not just the rules we've broken. Though our humanity doesn't excuse us from being obedient to God, it also isn't the end of the story to Him.

Jesus came to expose the stain,
erase the stain,
and elevate you above the stain.

No matter how good we think we are, we all have stains. If every one of us was required to wear our mistakes on the outside, none of us would be wearing white before *or* after Labor Day. If we're honest with ourselves, we can admit that our decisions, relationships, habits, and actions throughout the course of our life have most likely left dirt on our lives that doesn't seem to come off no matter how hard we try. Despite what we do to cover it up, somehow the deep stains—whether large or small—still show. Trying to wash away our own sins or dirt is like trying to paint over a moldy bathroom wall. No matter how many coats you apply, the black, telltale spots will eventually come back until the underlying issue is addressed. We can try to cover up the evidence, but the effects will still be harmful even if invisible. It's the same way with our lives. If we don't deal with the underlying issues behind the stains in our lives, it's only a matter of time before they start to show again and we start to experience the effects. We can try to cover it up with the coats of paint that make us feel better on the outside, like justifying, excusing, or defending, but it never quite erases the stains on the inside.

But Jesus came to expose the stain, erase the stain, and elevate you above the stain.

Expose, erase, and elevate? Now here's where the paradox of God begins to really unfold. Not only does God want to wash away the dirt from your life, He wants to position you and platform you as though you were never stained to begin with. He wants to wash away every trace of dirt so He can open doors for you that the world says should never be opened to you. He wants to bring you back to a place of innocence to use you in ways that others would say is impossible for someone like you. He wants to cleanse you of all unrighteousness so that He can give you back everything you lost, and then some.

But *why*? Why would God want to bless you when the rest of the world says He will curse you? Why would God justify you when everything you've done would warrant punishment?

Because God gets no glory in seeing His creation and His children suffer. God never intended to punish. He never wanted to penalize those He loves the most. It's not that obeying or disobeying God's standards don't have consequences, because they do. It's that God's *first* response has always been grace, not penalty.

PUNISHMENT OR PROTECTION?

This is a contradiction to the God most people know and understand. The widely accepted theology is that of a God waiting eagerly for us to break one of His rules so He can come swiftly to invoke punishment. Yet Scripture supports a different God, starting all the way back in Genesis.

In the first book of the Bible, God creates a utopia. Adam and Eve have everything at their disposal and they were free to enjoy it all without restraint. There was just one rule: don't eat from the tree of knowledge of good and evil. That's it. You'd think it wouldn't be too hard to follow just one rule. But Adam and Eve were tempted and the first stain soaked into the fabric of humanity. The rest of the story goes on to tell of God's punishment for their sins and the banishment from the perfect life they once knew. Not exactly the story of a God who extends grace first! It has been told and retold by generations as a model of what *not* to do. The result? Generations of young people are raised with the image of a God who is watching and waiting to kick us out at our first offense. But God didn't tell Adam that he was going to get kicked out of Eden if he ate from the tree of knowledge of good and evil. God's exact words were:

> And the LORD God commanded the man, saying, "Of every tree of the garden you may freely eat; but of the tree of the knowledge of good and evil you shall not eat, for in the day that you eat of it you shall surely die." (Genesis 2:16–17 NKJV)

So why didn't Adam and Eve immediately die? God's rule was specific. His command was explicit. His punishment was clear. But the God who breaks the rules stepped in to break His own rules to save them. And that's not all God does. Not only does He spare their lives, God also covers their sin by clothing them in their nakedness to demonstrate His forgiveness.

Even more paradoxical is God's final command to protect them by removing them from Eden. *What?* Wasn't it punishment, not protection, that kicked them out of the garden? The vast majority of people who know this biblical story often forget one small detail that shows a key part of God's heart for humanity. There wasn't just one tree in the garden; there were two. It wasn't the tree of knowledge of good and evil that got them removed; it was the other one:

> Then the LORD God said, "Behold, the man has become like one of Us, to know good and evil. And now, lest he put out his hand and take also of the tree of life, and eat, and live forever"—therefore the LORD God sent him out of the garden of Eden. (Genesis 3:22–23 NKJV)

What if I were to tell you God didn't remove them as punishment for eating from the tree of knowledge of good and evil? What if the truth is that He removed them from the garden so they wouldn't eat from the tree of life and live forever in the guilt, shame, and regret? This would mean God's primary focus was not to punish them but to protect them from the unending torment that would have ensued if He had allowed them to remain in Eden. This context shows it wasn't anger that drove them out; it was love. Love covered them. Love protected them. And love graced them. Though His punishment was evident, His grace for them was even more evident.

HIDING FROM GOD

I've known too many people who live with a constant fear that the dirt from their lives will get them "removed" from the life God originally intended for them. They don't see God as the God who will break the rules to save them, cover them, or protect them. They only see the punishment.

Is it possible you see only His correction and overlook His affection?

If you look back at your life, have there been times when all you felt was the punishment and anger of God instead of the love and forgiveness of His grace? Is it possible that maybe you missed His heart of grace because you were focused on His hand of justice? Is it possible you saw only His correction and overlooked His affection? Is it possible you felt alienated from God because of your stains, instead of covered and changed by His love and mercy? Our darkest, dirtiest moments seem to us like the worst times to find God, but they are actually the best ones! Our stained, dirty lives serve as a compass to point us back to God when we've tried every other option ourselves. Like Adam and Eve, we can try to hide from Him, but that only drives Him to come after us and ask, "Where are you?"

Today, where are you? Are you hiding behind mistakes that you can't get away from? Are you running from a past that keeps catching up to you? Are you buried behind mountains of lists, tasks, and deadlines to cover up the missing pieces of a life you wish you had?

Wherever you are, God is saying to you in a voice of forgiveness and unconditional love, "Where are you? Because I'm here for you."

Perhaps the most damaging aspect of hiding from God is that it keeps our perspective of God and His grace skewed by our own fear and guilt. As our personal choices and decisions begin to accumulate stains, soils, and blemishes that isolate us from God, He waits for the opportunity to break through the barriers that have come between us and Him. We struggle to get back up and dust ourselves off because we picture God as a distant stranger whose heart is inflexible, whose face is stern, and whose voice is silent. Too many of us have heard the condemning voice of the rules we've broken tell us over and over again that God can't use us if we're dirty, stained, and soiled. And so the dirt on our hands remains because we don't know what to do with it.

Once again, the story of David speaks to God's rule-breaking propensity.

Are you buried behind mountains of lists, tasks, and deadlines to cover up the missing pieces of a life you wish you had?

GREATNESS IN THE MESSY PLACES

It was with hands dirty from the field and clothes drenched in the stench of manure that David was summoned not for punishment, but for promotion. In fact, the prophet Samuel doesn't just call him; he waits until David arrives soiled from head to foot as though he were royalty.

> Then Samuel asked, "Are these all the sons you have?"
> "There is still the youngest," Jesse replied. "But he's out in the fields watching the sheep and goats."
> "Send for him at once," Samuel said. "We will not sit down to eat until he arrives." (1 Samuel 16:11)

David's father hesitated because of David's condition, but God didn't. When others aren't convinced you're good enough, clean enough, or holy enough to be promoted, God will still send for you anyway to promote you in front of all those who doubt you. And like David, God wants us to come with pure, honest admission of where we've been so we can trust Him with where we're going.

David's dirty promotion is a glimpse of a God that all of us need to see more of. You may walk into areas of your life and feel completely disqualified because of the stains in your own life, but we learn from David that our dirt doesn't determine His call. God sees past the markings of sin to position you in places you would never have imagined. To his brothers, David didn't belong at the table of honor, but to God, David didn't belong in the field. His family was content to leave him outside because their perspective of him was based only on who David was on the outside. The world and sometimes even the church will tell you that what's on the outside matters most, but God will break every rule to show you that He sees and thinks the opposite way of the world. God saw inside David, even though the outside stains broke His heart. David was only a young boy, but God saw every stain from his past, present, and future and, yet, He still called for him.

God knew that if He held to the rules, David wasn't the one to anoint. According to traditional rules, He would need to anoint Eliab, the firstborn, but God also knew that abiding by those same rules would promote a king no different than the one that He was demoting—Saul. God had no choice but to break the rules to break a pattern of leadership. Saul was the right guy on the outside, but wrong on the inside. David was the wrong guy on the outside, but the right guy on the inside. When God said He was going to promote a man after His own heart to replace Saul (see 1 Samuel 13:14), He was telling the world that He valued the inside of a man more than rules, which merely reflected the outside.

Patterns and traditions can hold you hostage to customs that keep you in assumption instead of anticipation. David *assumed* the prophet wasn't there for him so he didn't anticipate or expect anything for himself. His father assumed the firstborn would be called, not the youngest, so he didn't anticipate David being invited in. That's the danger with assumptions; they keep us outside of possibilities instead of at the table of promotion. It wasn't the prophet that kept David out. It was assumption and tradition that disqualified him.

The thing we have to remember is that David knew he was dirty. He knew he was disqualified. He knew he was the youngest, not the eldest. He knew he didn't go through the purification rituals that his brothers did. He knew he was stained. He wasn't in denial about his inadequacies, but he also wasn't in denial about his God's adequacies. When he was called for, he came. He didn't stay outside in doubt, fear, or shame. He trusted God enough to stand dirty in front of his father, his brother, and the prophet Samuel to admit that although he was stained on the outside, he was purified on the inside.

While his brothers stood clean after going through the purification process, David must have seemed detestable before them with hands and clothes stained deep with manure and dirt inside every crevice and crease. But I don't think that's how God saw him. I believe if we could have seen David's walk from the field to the table from God's perspective, we would have seen every past, future, and present sin fall off David with each step he took. When David finally got to the table, God saw a man dressed in the purity of His love and grace instead of a man stained from head to toe with dirt.

That's why, when the prophet Samuel saw him, he saw a man ready for promotion instead of condemnation.

The truth is, there is greatness in even the dirtiest of places.

When God sent His own Son to be born, He didn't come from a place we'd expect. He wasn't born in a nice suburban home with green grass or a hospital room with doting, attentive nurses. No, the Son of God was born in a *stable* and placed in a *manger*, where the foul stench of manure and waste permeated the air.

It was in that unimaginable, detestable, and filthy place that the Son of God breathed His first.

Why would God want to be associated with filth? Maybe because God knows our stench is really an opportunity for Him to get the glory from our story so the world can see that the only one who can clean us up is God.

Maybe it's because He knows our stains are merely an indication of our deep need of Him. Maybe it's because our stained lives are the perfect pieces in a story God is writing to the world that demonstrates His infinite love and desire to give us a second chance.

God isn't like the world. He sees beauty in the darkest of places and worth in the filthiest of lives. He wants us all to know that what has been discarded and disregarded because of disqualification has the potential to be accepted, approved, and announced because of His sanctification.

> ## He sees beauty in the darkest of places and worth in the filthiest of lives.

WHEN GOD SANCTIFIES THE SOILED

Most people, like David, don't need anyone to point out the stains in their life because they know them all too well. They already see the consequences of decisions that they carry with regret. They already see the places in their life that are broken and weak. They need someone to point them to a greater God who sees beyond all that. They need a glimpse of a greater love, a greater hope, and a greater future than their past.

"They" might mean your spouse, your children, your best friend, your parent, or even yourself. At some point in every person's life, we've all felt like a "they." Today, God wants every "they" to know that He is calling them to become "His." When we become His, we move past our own stains to see God's view of us from the inside out.

In the same way that you share the attributes of the family you've been born into, God wants you to share in His purity and authority as you become part of His family. He wants you to finally let go of the fragmented image you've carried of Him, and of yourself, and to instead see yourself the way He sees you. While you can't always see yourself for your stains, God can't see you without first seeing what His Son did on the cross to purify you.

Accepting what He's done as a greater reality than what you've done allows God to break down the walls of religious precepts to give you a genuine relationship with Christ. Through Christ, you can now find the courage and strength to accept the purification process that lovingly guides and corrects you, instead of excluding or punishing. And as this purification process happens, you begin to be open to things that you previously believed were closed to you. You start to see all things through the realm of possibility instead of through the scope of shame. And all the arguments and reasons why you shouldn't step out into the calling and promotion are now exposed as rules God is breaking to reveal why you *should*.

God wants you to now hear His voice calling you in from the field.

The paradox of God's sanctification is where most people stumble over and over again, whether they've never known God or known Him for their entire lives. In Eden, "human" was rewritten to mean "to err," and for too many, it became a graveyard of forgotten dreams, broken hearts, and defeated spirits. With every disappointment, every mistake, and every sin, we hide deeper behind the bushes of guilt and forget that God is not surprised or deterred by our sin. We can't truly fathom the depth of His redeeming call because we can't understand the paradox of His love. It's illogical and incomprehensible.

Yet our inability to grasp it doesn't negate it. He doesn't need our comprehension to demonstrate it. He doesn't need our understanding to reveal it. He needs only our belief in Him to do it!

When He calls you, don't stand in the field debating it. Follow David's example and come inside. Let His voice wash away every stain with every step you take toward Him. Let Him bring you before the haters, the doubters, and the naysayers to show off His plan that may not be understood, but still cannot be denied. Let Him be the God who breaks the rules for you right here, right now.

When you look at your life and see all the possibilities that you've been too afraid to walk toward, God wants you to now hear His voice calling you in from the field. He wants you to come inside from all the places you've been outside so that He can wash you, restore you, and promote you. He's calling you from last in line so He can position you to be *first*. The days of living in the stench of your past are over. No matter how much dirt you've lived with, it's time to come home. Forget everything that was done in the past so that you can move forward, while never forgetting the lessons it taught you.

You no longer have the stains that held you back, and, more importantly, you have the wisdom to never go back to what stained you. A once-stained life is now a wise life that has experienced firsthand not only the pain of regret, but also the power of redemption. A once-tarnished past now becomes a clear image of a God to a world that only knows His rules, not His grace.

An imperfect story becomes the perfect opportunity to tell the world that change is not only *possible*, but, when God rewrites your story, it is *inevitable*.

True freedom is found in submission.

6

WHO WANTS THE OIL?

"God's anointing doesn't make sense until it's
the only sense of God we have."
—Anonymous

It's one thing to know you've been called to accomplish great things, but it's an entirely different thing to have the resources, skill-sets, and abilities to pull off that greatness. Most people look at the task in front of them and then immediately look behind them at what they have to complete the job. With God, it works differently. He doesn't look at what you have in your toolbox. He looks beyond your now into your future, to plan and prepare to give you everything you need. And of all the things you'll ever need, His anointing is the one tool you can't live without.

The importance of the anointing is best understood through its biblical context. The Greek word for "anoint" is *chrio*, which means "to smear or rub with oil" and implies, "to consecrate." Throughout the Bible, people were anointed with oil to denote the blessing of God and indicate His call on their life. They were consecrated, or "set apart," for a specific purpose.

Today, anointing is still an integral part of God's call. The oil itself doesn't contain the blessing, but it serves as an outward symbol of the grace, approval, favor, and empowerment that God has placed on you and in you through His Holy Spirit. Being convinced God can and will break the rules for you opens your heart and mind to receive the outpouring of His oil. Having God's anointing is like having a direct-access pass to the life you were truly intended to live. His anointing is His affirmation that He is behind you and will give you what you need along the way. It leads you where you've never been before and gives you the insight to maneuver around obstacles so effortlessly, it doesn't make sense to you.

The anointing is a little like the yellow brick road.

Having God's anointing is like having a direct-access pass to the life you were truly intended to live.

When Dorothy in *The Wizard of Oz* went off to see the Wizard, she had to follow the yellow brick road. It led her to the Scarecrow, the Tin Man, the Cowardly Lion, and eventually the Wizard. Each new friend helped her along the journey until she arrived safely home in Kansas. Initially, she didn't know she needed a Scarecrow to know the need for wisdom, or a Tin Man to help her see the value of a heart, or a Cowardly Lion to give her the courage to carry on. But the yellow brick road led her to everything she needed, and even brought her protection when her enemy, the Wicked Witch, threatened to stop her from finishing what she started.

The anointing will lead you, like the yellow brick road led Dorothy, to people, places, positions, and protection that will help you to accomplish your call. Right now you might feel like Dorothy at the beginning of her journey: filled with questions, fears, and doubts. But the solution is the same for you as it was for her. Just follow—follow the anointing, follow God's call, and follow the path of oil.

CLOSE-UP ON GOD'S ANOINTING

God's anointing is simple. It's up to Him, it's from Him, and it's for Him. Easy. Let's look at each one of these in depth because the concept of the anointing is misunderstood by so many believers.

UP TO HIM

First and foremost, it is *His* choice on whom the anointing falls, not ours. More often than not, His choice is contrary to human reason. We look at who "should" have it while God looks at who wants it. He waits to pour it on those who are willing to fight to follow Him instead of wanting to fight so that others follow them. He calls and anoints based on what He sees, not what we see.

This truth frustrates people who feel entitled to the anointing because of what they've done or who they're affiliated with. However, in the Bible, the oil didn't fall on the experienced or socially acceptable; it spilled over to the spiritually hungry and overlooked. Today, the anointing still runs over rules and regulations to reach those with a lesser life résumé, so that they no longer stand overlooked. The oil becomes the assurance for you that in the midst of those who do not see in you what God sees, His anointing still comes to position you above every doubter, critic, and skeptic.

You've been taken from the field
of the forgotten and brought
to the gate of greatness.

The anointing is a great example of Jesus' words in the book of Matthew: *"For many are called, but few are chosen"* (Matthew 22:14 NKJV). You are not just called. You're chosen, consecrated, and set apart for Him, His call, and His plans for your life. You don't need to fight for the qualifications or approval to live the life you've been called to live. You already have it. It's already in you. You're not on the sidelines—hoping, wishing, dreaming of a greater life. You've been taken from the field of the forgotten and brought to the gate of greatness so that you can know without a shadow of a doubt that the oil has fallen on you. Stop looking for God to use someone else. It's you. Period. Let me say that again. It's you. It's you at home, you at work, you at school, you at church, you in every circle of influence. He placed you where you are, not so you could fail or give up, but so that He could work through you to make a difference for Him. Stop reading this book and thinking it's for someone else. God wrote this book for *you*, with you in mind, so that you would go after the more from Him that you've been running from. You're it and there is no better choice than you. His anointing, approval, and authorization is on *you*.

FROM HIM

Once you fully accept that it's His choice to call you and anoint you, the next rule God breaks is the one that prevents you from believing His anointing comes *from* Him and Him alone. People often say to me, "OK, even if I were to believe that God has anointed me, it has to be only because of x, y, or z." Our instinct is to try to logically explain why God has called and chosen to anoint us. We lean on the lie that it's because of this person or for that reason instead of fully resting in the truth that it's only because He has been waiting for the right moment to show you who you really are to Him. It's not because He collaborated with your Christian friend or your pastor to convince you to do more or be more. You have been on His mind since the beginning of time. He and He alone created you, formed you, called you, and anointed you with more already in you, so He alone is calling you to live out of that more. The Bible says it like this: *"Christ's anointing teaches you the truth on everything you need to know about yourself and him, uncontaminated by a single lie. Live deeply in what you were taught"* (1 John 2:27 MSG).

The anointing on you isn't dependent on who gives a good report of you and who doesn't. Even if no one sees you or gives a spiritual letter of recommendation on your behalf, God will still anoint you purely based on the spiritual reference His Son wrote for you on the cross. You are not forgotten or overlooked by Him and that's why He's brought you to this moment in your life. Stop looking for a holy hookup to get on the inside with God. Jesus already took care of it!

FOR HIM

After you've settled it in you that the anointing is up to Him and from Him, the next step is to accept that your anointing is *for* Him. The entire reason God anoints us is for Him. The anointing is His commissioning. Every brilliant idea and creative concept that He anoints you to bring forth is for the purpose that your life can serve as a billboard for the rules that He's broken in you. Through your story, the world sees a God unlike the one they've known. The anointing on your life surpasses the standards drawn by societal, cultural, and religious lines to paint a greater image of God. It paints over the tapestry of rules to serve as a reminder to those watching that He has qualified, chosen, sanctified, and anointed us for a greater purpose than our preexisting rules could allow. God uses your story to prove there are no rules—past, present, or future—that can limit the commissioning anointing of the Holy Spirit in your life.

The entire reason God anoints us is for Him.

When the anointing oil fell on David, his entire life changed. He went from being a seventeen-year-old shepherd boy whom everyone had forgotten to being the next king of Israel. Over the years, I've wondered if David had any idea how symbolic the anointing oil was on his life that day Samuel showed up at his father's house. Part of me thinks he couldn't have grasped the enormity and significance of the anointing oil at such a young age, but another part of me remembers that David was a shepherd. And as a shepherd, David would have used oil to protect his flock. Sheep were at high risk for lice and insects that would infest their wool and even burrow into the sheep's ears, eventually causing death. To ward off insects, shepherds would pour oil onto the sheep's head, making the wool too slippery for an insect to enter the ear canal. Oil was a shepherd's way of protecting and preserving the flock. When he was anointed, David may have felt like one of God's sheep, being protected from all the lies that threatened to creep into his ears and kill the future God had called him to. He must have known that the oil flowing from Samuel's flask to his head was the fullness of God's affirmation over his life. His brothers saw it. His father saw it. And though they had overlooked him before, they would never overlook him again.

WHEN THE ANOINTING FALLS ON THE OVERLOOKED

Sam didn't plan on living in the background of life, but that's where he ended up. He could build anything with the expertise of a skilled engineer. I remember giving him hand-drawn ideas for set designs on a napkin or spare piece of paper and watching him create it with his bare hands with far greater excellence than I could ever imagine. He was more than gifted; he was *anointed* to build. He had one of those stories that you almost couldn't believe was true. He had come to our church and gotten saved after years of battling drugs and violence. To those in his past, he was a criminal, but to us, he was nothing like that. We saw him as a quiet, generous man who had turned his life around to become one of the key volunteers building a chapter in the history of our church.

One day I got a call that broke my heart. Unbeknownst to us, Sam was here in America undocumented. His past choices had caught up to him and he was being deported. No goodbyes. No prayerful sendoff. No grateful departure. Just like that, Sam was gone.

Quickly, he drifted back to a lifestyle of drugs to drown away the pain of having to say goodbye to the life and son he'd left behind in America. He felt hopeless, lost, and forgotten by God. He tried to stay in contact and find a church in Tijuana, but was too brokenhearted to keep going forward. He slowly accepted the blaring, relentless lie that God had left him and abandoned him. He recklessly lived the next eight years without concern for his life or future and ended up in a prison in Tijuana. He genuinely believed he was going to die a prisoner and would never set foot in our church again.

For almost a decade Sam felt forgotten, but God wasn't done with his story.

I had lost track of Sam over the years and had no idea that he was a prisoner. All I knew was that God was opening doors for our church to build a church inside a prison in Tijuana. The first day I walked into the prison to meet with the warden, Sam was not on *my* mind—but he was on God's. I walked through the security gates onto an empty lot of dirt, and I heard my name called out. "Pastor Sergio!" I turned around and saw the face of a man I hadn't seen in years. Sam looked at me with tears in his eyes, and at that moment, I knew exactly why God had brought me there.

God had not forgotten Sam. He had not let go of His plan to use him to build His kingdom. God had brought me to a prison in another country to build a church from dirt to remind Sam that God wasn't done building hope and faith in him. By all accounts, we were not supposed to be building a church in a Tijuana prison. There were too many rules to count that should have stopped us. But there I was, standing in God's dream for not just Sam, but for the thousands of Sams in that prison who believed God had forgotten them as well.

Sam skillfully helped us build a church inside the prison the same way he had helped us build a church in San Diego over ten years before. No longer is the prison a symbol of loss for him. Now it represents a God who broke every rule to rebuild his hope, courage, and faith. Every week he serves alongside our team to minister to the inmates who believe God has forgotten them. He is doing what he never thought possible. No matter how far Sam got from God, no matter what rules and borders tried to limit his destiny, and no matter how many times he had tried to give up, God never gave up on Sam. Today, Sam knows he'll never be forgotten by the God who broke the rules to find him.

IT'S NOT THE END

Whatever prison you're living in isn't the end of your life. You're not going to die in a prison of a job that you hate. You're not going to die incarcerated in a marriage that no longer has hope. You're not going to die imprisoned by fear, worry, and loss. God has already laid out a blueprint of hope to build inside the prison of your heart, mind, and soul a reminder that He sees you now just like He saw you before. Your life isn't the sum result of what you've done or who've you been. Your life is the culmination of His anointing mixed with His grace to protect and guide you through every season. If you will let Him pour His oil on you right now, it will be what carries you through the highs and lows and ups and downs that don't make sense to you, but make sense to Him. He knows where you're going and why He needs you there. As Sam's life shows, His anointing changes the prisons of our lives from places of pain to places of peace.

Your life isn't the sum result of what you've done or who've you been.

What rules do you need God to break so that *you* can believe in *Him* the way *He* believes in *you?* What lies have crept into your mind that God needs to dispel? What places of pain does God need to transform for you to trust His promotion?

When I first heard God tell me He was the God who breaks the rules, I was more than hesitant to go public with His revelation. I didn't want to stand before thousands and say the unthinkable. I didn't want to write a book about a rule-breaking God because I knew what would follow. A book about the paradoxes of God was bound to challenge people because it was challenging me. I fought with God, fought with myself, fought with publishers, and fought with my team to write a different book, but God wouldn't stop speaking to me. I would try to preach a different sermon while traveling around the world, and God wouldn't let me. Over and over again, He kept bringing me back to the biblical concept that I wanted to avoid. He kept telling me to look at how He had worked in the lives of those in the Bible. I asked myself over and over again, *How could the book of God's rules be where God leads me to see Him breaking the rules?* It was a paradox to me, but I kept obeying. And God kept whispering to me a sentence that I couldn't run from forever: "Sergio, I broke the rules to find you and I need you to help Me break the rules to find others."

His words were not ones I could deny. My life is a story of rules broken by God's grace, and I couldn't hide from that truth. I'm not the son of generational privilege or prestige. I don't come from a lineage of pastors, authors, or speakers. I don't have a résumé with degrees from an Ivy League university. What I do have is a biography that includes two immigrant parents who spoke little to no English but spoke fluently the language of faith, family, integrity, and honor. I have a life story that includes sitting among some the greatest men of faith the world has ever known, speaking at some of the most hallowed halls in America, and pastoring one of the greatest churches in the country for almost two decades alongside my wife and family.

God is the only reason I have been able to achieve any success in my life and He is the One who positions and platforms me in places I have no qualifications to be. God is the One who took the young gang member in me and anointed me for more. God is the One who took the businessman in me and formed a man who only cares about my Father's business. God is the One who took my wanderings as a seventeen-year-old kid and anointed me with a mission to turn hearts.

His anointing changes the prisons of our lives from places of pain to places of peace.

God is the One who broke the rules to call me, sanctify me, and anoint me—not for my own plans and purposes, but for His. And He didn't do it just for me. He wants to do it for anyone who wants the anointing more than anything else in this life. It's for anyone who will fight tooth and nail to believe in a greater God than they've known or heard of before. It's for every person, young and old, who will rise up and refuse to be defined by anything other than His call on their life. It's for everyone who will believe in a God who can and will break the rules to find them. Everything that has defined you before this moment doesn't have to define the rest of your life. No matter how you started, God can finish your story the way He originally intended it to be. You don't need to come from greatness to be born into greatness.

You don't need an ancestry of prestige to be associated with prominence. You don't need a flawless past to have a favored future. Your faith in God attributes all of His perfection to your imperfection. He changes everything to change your past, present, and future.

But it doesn't happen overnight; it's a process.

You don't need a flawless past to have a favored future.

WAITING IT OUT

When you look at the story of David, it's easy to forget that while he was anointed king as a young boy, he didn't actually become king until he was thirty years old. (See 2 Samuel 5:4.) That's over a decade of time between the time God called and anointed him and the realization of that call.

What would that decade of waiting look like for you? Would you have doubts after a year? How about five years? Ten years? Would you begin to question the validity of that day the prophet showed up at your house? Would you have the same expectancy and anticipation at thirty as you did at seventeen? If we're honest, we have to admit that every one of us would wonder if maybe we heard wrong. We would all think we might have missed it along the way.

What happens from the time we're called and anointed to the time we see the fulfillment of the call is what I call "the process." And no one escapes the process. We all have to take the journey to go from David to King David. This is where I've seen some crash and burn and others thrive and fly. It all depends on how you walk out the process of your anointing.

David had to walk out insecurities, jealousy, fear, loneliness, submission, and opposition. He had to mature into the throne before he could be given the throne. There were countless times along the way that David could have given up, walked away, denied his call, or lost hope, but he grew *into* God instead of away from God. Our willingness to want the oil and wait for the oil forms in us what God wants through a process that can't be completed by rules, but only by relationship.

When we look further into David's life through Scripture, we see that he was anointed three times in his life. The first time was as a young teenager when God revealed his identity publicly. (See 1 Samuel 16:13.) The second time was after Saul's death when David was publicly anointed to step into his destiny and take his place as king. (See 2 Samuel 2:4.) It was there that God revealed his confirmation publicly. The third time was when God expands David's influence and authority to all of Israel. (See 2 Samuel 5:3.) This anointing publicly demonstrated God's covenant not only with David but with the nation as a whole. Before this final anointing, Israel was broken, divided, and weak. Through his third anointing, David was able to unite the nation to God and to each other, painting an image of God and His anointing that looks very much like the shape of the cross. However, it was a process: before reaching an expanded influence, he had to undergo the valley of humility and then even the shadow of death as consequences for his sins as king. What was birthed in David's first anointing died in his second anointing and was later resurrected in his third anointing. Yet at each anointing and during each season in between, God was with David and never failed to remind him that He had not changed His mind.

> ### What was birthed in David's first anointing died in his second anointing and was later resurrected in his third anointing.

This process in David is not just evident in David's life. It's part of your journey as well.

Today, you may feel like the young kid who is hearing God's call and feeling God's anointing fall for the first time. Or you may be the thirty-year-old stepping into your second anointing without any idea of how to walk out it out. Or you may have even lived for years knowing God has anointed you, but are still fighting to overcome the division, resistance, and obstacles from the past. Regardless of what stage of God's process of growth you are in, know that *more* is on its way to you. No matter where you are in the process of discovering and growing in your anointing with God, God has not forgotten or overlooked you. Where you are and what you're experiencing is not the end. Don't lose your *want* for the anointing. God will never pour His anointing on those who don't want it—all of it. He looks for those who want the oil, but also for those who are willing to pay whatever price it takes to get it and grow in it.

Some of you have been paying a price that no one has seen for longer than you can remember. You've been hungry for the anointing oil for so long that you've wondered if it's still worth it anymore; if God still wants to give you more; if He hasn't perhaps forgotten what He promised.

I assure you, God sees the price you're paying to hold on to a call that hasn't come to pass yet. He knows the anguish you've been going through to believe in a promise that is still on its way. He hasn't forgotten the day He called you from the field. He hasn't forgotten the public display of His affection and approval washing over you. He hasn't forgotten you. You may feel like giving up, but God is still with you. You still have another anointing coming if you will just keep moving forward. Don't lose your fight for the anointing. It's closer than you think.

THE ANOINTED LIFE

It may not make sense why God chose you when others forgot about you. It may not be comprehensible how God can pour out an oil that both blesses you and costs you. It may not be logical to you how God can publicly promote you while privately processing you. This is the paradox of stepping into an anointed life.

It's not going to make sense to you because it's redefining you, your future, and the rules that have stood in the way. God starts by breaking the rules to redefine who He is to you and then leads you through the journey of breaking the rules to redefine who you are to Him. The freedom to know Him, hear Him, and follow Him without any limitations can now begin to breathe life again back into old dreams, past hopes, and forgotten promises. Instead of a set of rules that leave you with a "should have" or "should have not," God gives you a new canvas of faith to rewrite "what if" and "what will be." It's the beginning of a life that's no longer marked by rules, regulations, and limitations, but now marked by the purpose, power, and promise in His anointing. He has not forgotten you and He has not changed His mind about you.

Inside your life is the oil of His anointing to shape you, form you, position you, platform you, and protect you. You're not waiting for it. You already have it! Live in that reality and let it overpower the reality of a broken system of rules that has held you back from believing, anticipating, and living out God's call.

It's you. It's always been you. God just wants to know: *do you want the oil?*

There is victory in loss.

7

SWEET VINDICATION

"I consider myself a crayon.... I may not be your favorite color but one day you'll need me to complete your picture."
—Lauryn Hill

When Rosa Parks refused to move to the back of the bus on December 1, 1955, she didn't know her name would become synonymous with one of the greatest civil rights movements in history. All she knew was that she had been moved around, pushed around, and bossed around one too many times because of the color of her skin.

She wasn't trying to initiate a city-wide protest or a 381-day bus boycott. She was just trying to get home after a long day at work.

She wasn't trying to rewrite history, but when an opportunity presented itself for her to either bow down or rise up, she chose to rise up. Her one small act forced the nation to realize that if they disagreed with a law or rule, they had the power to try to change it.

In David's life, it wasn't a bus driver who stood between him and his future. It was a giant. After David was called and anointed in front of his family, it had to have been pretty difficult for him at home. He most likely wasn't understood or liked very much by the brothers who had been passed up for the crown. It's probably safe to say that when the Philistines started a war, David was *not* the one his brothers wanted with them on the front lines. Once again, David is overlooked and left behind in the field while his brothers go out to fight. But an errand from his father places him right in the middle of an opportunity, much like Rosa Parks was placed.

David's father asks him to take food to his brothers in the Israelite camp. So here is David just trying to deliver food when he hears the taunting and mocking of a giant, the Philistine hero, looking down on him, every other Israelite, and most importantly, God Himself. No one believed God would use David to go after Goliath. Using a kid with no war experience was against the rules of war. At that moment, David had to choose to let himself be used to break the rules and not be moved by what the giant or his brothers were saying. He had to choose to agree with God, even if it put him in disagreement with everyone else. He had the opportunity to bow down to Goliath or to rise up, and he chose to rise up.

His brothers called him prideful and nosy. (See 1 Samuel 17:28.) King Saul called him too young. (See verse 33.) And Goliath called him a joke with a stick. (See verse 43.) But God called him a champion.

Whenever God breaks the rules on your behalf to use you in ways that are illogical and incomprehensible to others, there will be moments when who you are becoming clashes with who others want you to become. They'll ask you to go back to who you were, like David's brothers did when they told him to go home. They'll tell you to be more like them, like Saul did when he tried to put his own armor on David. They'll curse you and mock you, like Goliath did as David ran up to him. They'll do anything they can to get you to move from your position so that the one who is more deserving, more accepted, or more privileged can take your place. Don't do it. Don't buy into the lie that it's not you. Don't give up the seat God gave you. Don't let your disagreement with them get you to disagree with God. If you will stay in your seat no matter what comes at you, you'll end up changing more than just you. You'll start a wave of change in others who don't know how to raise their voices yet, but who are learning how because of you.

The stance you take with God at the expense of being despised as a rule-breaker unwittingly gives others permission to break the rules that have held them hostage as well. It's more than just victory; it's *vindication*. Vindication, true vindication, is not about proving you are right; it's about God proving to the world He is right. He was right in choosing you. He was right in anointing you. He was right in promoting you. And He was right in breaking the rules to do it.

> Vindication is not about proving you are right; it's about God proving to the world He is right.

THE GROUND OF VINDICATION

Too often we give up on our story because we don't like the chapter we're on. We feel as though, if God really did call us from the field to the throne, we'll never have to go back to the field again. That's not true. The power of vindication is not in what you leave behind, but instead in what you take into the future as proof of how far you've come. The field, or the past, was not a place David looked at in shame. It was a place of victory and vindication reminding him every day that God loved him so much, He was willing to call him from the lowest place to the highest place. In the field, God's reality overshadowed his reality. What was once a place of pain, rejection, and loneliness had now become God's place of promise.

The ground of vindication for most of us is stained with tears of pain and etched with prints in the dirt from worn knees bowed in prayer. My wife and I know that ground. Years ago I watched God give my wife, Georgina, a ground of vindication that bore a pain greater than any she'd ever known.

A few years after we started our church, Georgina and I got the news that we were expecting. We were ecstatic from day one, and every day Georgina's face glowed more and more with joy at the promise of another child. She was the embodiment of life and it overflowed to every area of our lives. We were in love with each other, our family, our church, and our future. It was a moment in life when God's favor seemed to be coming from every direction. We told our growing church and publicly welcomed the excitement and bliss of a new De La Mora baby. Weeks went by and every Sunday my wife led us into worship with her growing belly more and more visible. It was one the happiest times in my life, watching her worship with freedom and pure abandonment before God. She had never looked more beautiful to me and I will never forget the joy that radiated from her.

But like a gorgeous sunset bursting out one last bright ray of light before descending into the horizon, darkness was coming.

She had just entered her second trimester when she miscarried. In the blink of an eye, our hopes, dreams, and joy were gone. The anguish on my wife's face as she sobbed in my arms was more pain-filled than any expression I had ever seen on her before. I had no words as I held her, my own tears falling. There is no logic in pain that raw and there is no comfort that can ease the ache of a loss so great. Her most private pain was public before her heart could even begin to catch up with what her mind was struggling to grasp. Our family and church immediately rallied alongside us and poured their love out on us in waves too great to hold back, but nothing could heal the deep inner wound in my wife's heart. She held tight to God and never uttered a single word in protest to His will, but the pain of losing this precious life was unbearable for her.

Racked with sadness, she turned to the only thing she knew that would heal her heart—worship. Worship became her refuge. It was the only place where she could bare her soul and walk away a little bit more whole each time. She stepped onto the stage with a vulnerable transparency before God and led our church through lyrics and choruses of hope, faith, and triumph. With every word she sang, life began to flow back into her heart as she bravely allowed God to use her deepest, private pain for His public purposes. Women who had endured the same heartache were drawn to her and borrowed from her strength as they found the courage to keep moving forward. Women who had never had children leaned on her faith to believe as they held on to their own promises. Women who had never known her pain stood with her in support and encouragement as they silently wept in gratitude for their own, healthy children. It was a bond of sisterhood that every woman needs and it radiated from her courage to publicly walk out her healing.

That platform of worship became a vindication ground where she warred for a promise, a future, and a hope that spoke louder than her overwhelming grief. It represented a posture of victory, not defeat. It mirrored her faith for healing after the loss of our child and represented a platform of surrender for her, building faith into our church that couldn't have happened any other way. Many people were worried that she had returned to leading worship too quickly, but she knew that it was only through God's leading and strength that she even had the desire to go back.

It's absurd that God would use a public platform to heal a private pain, but that's what He did in my wife's life. Even as she walked through it, I'm sure she had doubts and questions she never vocalized, but she remained firm that God's will would be done. She refused to give up hope for the miracle that God would turn her pain and loss around for a greater good. And she was right. Three years later, my wife gave birth to a healthy, happy, full-of-life baby girl. We named her Miracle Joy because that's exactly what God gave us. He took the insurmountable pain of loss and transformed it into a miracle of joy. Those days, weeks, and years of praising Him in her darkest moments allowed God to give Georgina a platform of vindication publicly and privately. Miracle Joy is our reminder that what we sow in pain, we reap in joy.

Years afterward, Miracle Joy, after experiencing death through the loss of her grandfather and grandmother, told us she had been thinking about our baby in heaven. She was wondering why she was born and the baby before her wasn't. She was trying to wrap her young mind around a confusing, scary concept like death. She needed an answer to the questions of her heart that only God could provide. And in His infinite faithfulness, He gave our young daughter an answer that carried more insight than I've ever heard any young child utter: "God told me 'I just wasn't ready yet.'" To her, the baby that we never held in our arms was sent to prepare our hearts for the one we would hold—her. This beautiful conversation between her and God brought peace not only to her little heart, but to ours as well.

He broke our rules about Him by breaking our hearts.

HE WALKED IT FIRST

Before experiencing this vindication ground, we never imagined God's method of giving people hope for their own miracle would be through our own story of loss. If we're honest, we didn't want to know this part of God. We wanted to know Him as the One who gives, not the One who takes away. We didn't know how to believe in a God who works through pain, grief, and loss. To us, the God who loves so infinitely could not possibly be the same God who allows us to grieve so deeply. Our rules about God were that He would protect us from loss, not walk us through it. We didn't truly know the God of healing and restoration until we had no other God to lean on.

The truth is, He broke our rules about Him by breaking our hearts.

In the darkest parts of life, God won't fit into our molds of logic, understanding, and reasoning, and it will feel like God has abandoned us. We will begin to doubt His plan and purposes for our life. We will feel like He's broken the rules of His character so we feel entitled to break the rules of our commitment to Him. But God never promised that we wouldn't endure loss. His Word teaches us the opposite in the gospel of John:

> *I have told you all this so that you may have peace in me. Here on earth you will have many trials and sorrows. But take heart, because I have overcome the world.* (John 16:33)

God's promise to us is not that we will be able to avoid suffering and pain, but that we will have peace and victory over the pain. When heartache comes our way, it's easier to see it as God's punishment than as His process toward perfection. Our rules tell us life gets hard because of a flaw in His character rather than because His method is working through the flaws in ours. Our rules see loss as His abandonment rather than as an opportunity to bring us closer to Him. Our rules whisper to us that we're victims instead of victors. Lies begin to fill our hearts and divide us from relationship with Him. Lies like:

If God really loved me and cared for me, this wouldn't have happened.

If God is who He said He is, I wouldn't be going through this.

If God is so good, bad things wouldn't keep happening to me.

The truth is, God works through the good, the bad, and the ugly to show us He is for us, with us, and beside us. We just have to be willing to let Him walk us through the rest of our story.

If Georgina had decided to stop moving forward in her relationship with God because of her loss, she would have never held Miracle Joy in her arms. Even when we don't see all the pieces, we must continue to trust Him to finish the puzzle that doesn't make sense to us. Regardless of how painful and brutal some of the pieces in your life have been, there are still pieces in His hand that He's waiting to place. And when the picture of your life is displayed for all the world to see, it will tell a story of faith, conviction, and vindication in God that no one will be able to deny.

Whatever field or platform you're standing on right now is the place God has called you to war for your own promises. It will not be the place that you lay down and die. It will not be the place where your pain is louder than your faith. It will not be the place where everything you believed in is lost. It will be the place that God reveals to you and to the watching world that He sees you, He defends you, and He vindicates you.

One of the things I love most about the God we are rediscovering on this journey is that He takes a principle of truth like that of His vindication and He walks it out *first* to show us He can be trusted. When someone tells us they're going to do the impossible, our first response is usually, "Show me." Knowing this, God always goes before us to show us that He will never ask us to do anything He isn't willing to do first. God knew what it felt like to lose something so precious. He knew what it meant to have the haters, doubters, and liars think they had won. He knew what it looked like to see what He loved most come to an end. When His Son, Jesus, was on the cross, it looked like God had lost. There was so much pain surrounding Jesus' death that it had to feel as though God had forsaken His Son, especially if you were at the foot of the cross hearing these words: *"And about the ninth hour Jesus cried out with a loud voice, saying, 'Eli, Eli, lama sabachthani?' that is, 'My God, My God, why have You forsaken Me?'"* (Matthew 27:46 NKJV).

The end was not the end to God; it was just the beginning.

All those who had walked with Jesus, believed in Jesus, and loved Jesus must have believed that if God had forsaken His Son, then God could forsake any of them. Their worst case scenario had just become their worst case reality. The cross, in that moment, was a part of the puzzle that was covered in defeat, in loss, and in sorrow. His disciples and followers must have felt broken by grief, humiliation, and loss. They hid and mourned in private to avoid persecution and tried to figure out what to do next. It took three days for the next piece of the puzzle to be put in place. Yes, God had allowed His Son to die a brutal, public death, but He had also vindicated Him to the world through a miraculous, public resurrection.

The end was not the end to God; it was just the beginning.

Jesus took the power of death and forced it to succumb to the greater promise of life—life for all of us. His resurrection opened the door for our resurrection. His ending became our beginning. His victory set up our vindication. For us, the cross is now the universal symbol of life, not death.

BECAUSE REAL LIFE HURTS

How many times in your life have you felt like you were face to face with your worst-case reality and wanted to give up and walk away? Maybe you're in that place right now and you're ready to throw the towel in because you can't see the next puzzle piece to your life. God wrote this book to tell you that this is not your end; this is just your beginning. Give Him permission to break the rules of loss, death, and grief to birth a new chapter in your life by making the choice to not quit. Don't go into hiding or avoid people and conversations. God isn't done placing all the pieces in your life.

It may be through tears and faith the size of a mustard seed that you hold on, but keep holding on. It may be through a broken heart that you keep trusting God, but keep trusting Him. It might even be through anger that you fight with God to understand His plan, but keep talking to Him. Too often we hold back raw, honest conversations with God out of fear that we have to approach Him only through perfect Christian rhetoric.

Real answers to real problems are found in a real relationship with a real God.

The reality is real answers to real problems are found in a real relationship with a real God.

A relationship with God *should* look messy and complex because we, in our humanity, are imperfect. If our relationships with family and friends are marked by a wide range of emotions, why is it so difficult to fathom a relationship with God would be the same—with joy, bliss, delight, but also disappointment, frustration, and anger? Over the years of growing in my relationship with Him, I have fought with God. I know that's not a typical pastor speech, but it is the honest one. I have fought with Him to find me, remind me, and align me when I struggle to hear and see Him in the day to day. I have fought with Him to remind me that He's called me to this life when the road is uncertain. I have fought with Him to correct my errors or confirm my wisdom so that I don't hold on to wrong ideas that I think are right or let go of right ideas that I think are wrong. I have fought with Him to give me the strength to see the infuriating injustices around me the way He sees them so that I don't live angry and bitter. I have fought with Him to convince me again that His love for me is greater than my weakness, faults, and failures and that His plan to use my life greatly will never change.

By the end, I'm crying, not fighting, and I hear His voice above every argument in me. Not every conversation is that intense, of course, but the point is that you cannot be afraid to let Him break your rules of how to talk with Him. Through these real conversations, I came to know parts of His heart that I would never have known if I had hidden my heart from Him.

JOB'S VINDICATION

If there was anyone in the Bible who had a just cause to be angry with God and long for vindication, it was Job. His life went from the dream life to a nightmare in an instant. It wasn't his unrighteousness that led to his suffering; it was his *righteousness* that opened the door. Talk about a paradox. Job did everything right, and he ended up losing everything he loved, at least temporarily—but Job didn't know that it would be temporary.

It started with a conversation between Satan and God. Satan argued that Job only loved God because God favored him, blessed him, and protected him. Remove the outpouring of God, Satan said, and Job would have an outpouring of curses for God. As absurd as it may sound, God agreed to let Job endure great loss at the hands of Satan to prove Job's love and relationship with God was real. Why would God ever let that happen? Why would God let Job intentionally go through hardship and suffering? Where is the merciful, just God that Job serves now? The idea of God withholding from us because we give Him everything is a paradox; it's outright illogical, absurd, and unreasonable. Yet, God was confident that Job would not only survive, he would *still* not curse Him.

Satan leaves him penniless, sitting in sackcloth and ashes, scraping at the terrible boils on his skin with a bit of broken clay. Now, when I read the book of Job, I don't read anywhere that Job curses God—even after God takes away his children, his wealth, his livelihood, his cattle, his health, and his strength. What I do read is Job's complaining and questioning.

In my mind, as I'm reading halfway through the book of Job, my impression is that Job failed to pass the test. As his suffering continues, his complaining increases to the point that he questions God's character. When

God finally answers Job out of a whirlwind, He spends three chapters educating Job on the supremacy of His character and His unchanging plans and, in the end, Job is repentant and remorseful for his onslaught of complaints. What I love is that while God challenged Job's incorrect theologies and mindsets, He never once removed His presence from him. He stayed in the conversation with Job until Job was able to see a side of God he had never known. He undid the erroneous rules in Job to convince him that He was committed to Job even if the circumstances dictated otherwise. At the end of Job's story, we see the vindication of God that no one, not even Satan, could deny. Job says, "I had only heard about you before, but now I have seen you with my own eyes. I take back everything I said.... So the LORD blessed Job in the second half of his life even more than in the beginning" (Job 42:5–6, 12).

It wasn't that God was permissive of Job's complaints as much as He was patient with his character. Job's story is an educational one for all of us. This truth gives us the framework to grow under God's patience and grace for us as we walk through the process of letting Him break our rules in the moments that break our hearts.

If you've been struggling to give God a second chance in your life because of all that you've lost, maybe you've been looking at this season of your life through the wrong filter. Your faith in Him, not the flaws in you, is what brought this crossroads to your life. His love, not His abandonment, is what has brought you to the place where you finally see Him with your own eyes. And just like Job, the paradox of your pain is that vindication will certainly come in the end.

WHEN THE WORLD CANNOT DENY YOUR STORY

Some of you know what it's like to have your story change overnight, whether it be positively or negatively. You've felt the pain of loss so great that it changed every part of you from that point on. Others of you have felt the elation of promotion that came from unexplainable favor so unimaginable that it changed you forever. Regardless of your experiences, God's promises for you are still the same. There is much more God wants to give you in the latter days of your life than the beginning. Trust that the process God has you on will lead you not only to the road of restoration, but also to the place of vindication. The end of your story will not be one of failure or loss. God's stories never end that way. He loves to have the final word in the last chapter of your life so that His last word brings forth the vindication that the world cannot deny.

Undoubtedly it may not feel like you're on your way to vindication today, but remember these stories of the faith that has triumphed. Remember the stories of men and women who experienced great pain and then great victory. Remember the lives of Rosa Parks, David the shepherd, Job, and Georgina De La Mora, people who didn't give up until they saw God use their pain for His plans and purposes.

Most of all, remember the life of Jesus and of those who followed Him who thought they'd lost all hope on the cross. Never did they imagine that the cross, which represented so much anguish and suffering, would one day be the symbol of vindication for generations to come.

The cross is the ultimate paradox when it comes to God's triumph over the enemy. It was the most treacherous loss that equated to the most glorious gain. It serves as a statement of truth that God can and will restore everything that was lost in our lives if we will let Him work out the process of resurrection in us. When you feel stretched from end to end, nailed by the mistakes of your past, and ridiculed by those who don't understand who you are, remember that, just like Jesus, you, too, will rise again. You, too, will step out of pain and sorrow to enter into a greater purpose, a greater promise, and a greater plan than you can imagine. You, too, will be vindicated.

Our failure is His success.

8

FALLING FORWARD

"Every stumble is not a fall, and every fall does not mean failure."
—Oprah Winfrey

Dramatic falls can sometimes end up as dramatic victories.

Just ask Shaunae Miller. In the 2016 summer Olympics, the Bahamian runner took her place on the starting blocks at the stadium in Rio De Janeiro, Brazil, and waited for the gun to go off to start the 400-meter finals. Her eye was on competitor Allyson Felix who was attempting to be the only American woman in track history to win five gold medals. With both athletes determined to cross the finish line first, the final steps of the race proved to be one audiences would tell over and over again. For most of the race, Miller was in the lead but Felix steadily gained until, right before the finish, they were running side-by-side. Breathless and desperate for a win, Miller lunged headfirst and dove across the finish line in a dramatic and unconventional finish. Was it a stumble? Did she throw herself forward intentionally? Did she just dive for first place? Shocked, everyone waited for the results while Miller lay on the track gasping for breath. Seconds later, the young Bahamian was announced the winner with a margin of victory of only .07 seconds ahead of her opponent.

Miller may not have won gold in a traditional fashion, but she proved that a stumble can still lead to glorious victory. Her fall forward pushed her torso .07 seconds ahead for the win. If she hadn't stumbled, she would have had a silver medal around her neck instead of a gold.

What if I were to say to you that God is asking you and me to do the same thing today? In life, each one of us is desperately running toward a promise, and God wants to know if we will dive headfirst and heart-first, even if it means stumbling publicly. Will we risk losing everything to lean wholeheartedly toward our destiny? Will we break out of traditional methods to reach untraditional victories? Our willingness to say yes to God's unorthodox methods opens the door to a life that is far more precious than gold.

RUTH'S STUMBLE

Ruth's life, like David's, was insignificant until she stumbled into her destiny. She was a widow, a woman, and a foreigner. As a widow, she had no social, spiritual, or economic respect. As a woman with no inheritance, she had nothing to look forward to but pain and sorrow. As a foreigner, she was seen as a stranger with no rights to the land. Faced with the decision of either going back to her family or going forward with her mother-in-law, Naomi, she chose to stumble headfirst and heart-first into the unknown with Naomi. *"Don't ask me to leave you and turn back,"* she told Naomi. *"Wherever you go, I will go; wherever you live, I will live. Your people will be my people, and your God will be my God"* (Ruth 1:16). Ruth was running toward a future that didn't promise her a victory, but she chose to lean in and fall forward anyway.

To truly understand the magnitude of Ruth's decision, let's look at her background. Ruth was a Moabite in Old Testament Israel. Now, the Moabites were among the most sexually perverse tribes, even from their beginning as the progeny of an incestuous relationship between Lot and his oldest daughter. They were pagans who did not worship the God of Israel that Ruth's husband and mother-in-law served, and they were looked at as disgusting and inferior. The Jewish culture of her husband's Israelite lineage would have maintained strict rules and laws that viewed Ruth's presence as an offense to their God.

After her husband passed away, Ruth was not only a Moabite, she was a widowed Moabite, adding insult to injury in her story. She was now cursed in her future and in her past. She would have been targeted, harassed, and beleaguered. She had every reason to go back to her family, her gods, and her country, but she didn't. Even though she didn't know where it would lead her, she chose to follow her mother-in-law and mother-in-law's God into the unknown.

Her decision was the difference between stumbling forward into victory and shrinking back in defeat. As Ruth chooses to work toward her future in the fields, gathering leftover crops to sustain herself and her mother-in-law, the Bible tells us she "just so happened" to work at the field of a man who would change her entire life. (See Ruth 2:1–3.) Boaz had the resources, the reputation, and the respect of the entire city—and could have had the attention of any woman. Yet, it isn't Ruth who notices him, but he who notices the stumbles of Ruth—a Moabite, a widow, and a foreigner picking up wheat that his paid laborers left behind. It's like a modern-day CEO walking to his lucrative business to promote, not the employee of the month, but the homeless beggar digging for scraps in the dumpster behind the offices. It's preposterous and absurd, but it's exactly what happened to Ruth. Boaz extends kindness to her and offers her protection from the onslaught of insults she has no doubt endured.

But Boaz is not able to just marry Ruth. In their culture, in order to marry Ruth and redeem her story, he would need to first ask the relative who had rightful position "next in line" as Ruth's kinsman-redeemer to take her as his wife. This was a provision in Israelite law so that widows without children could carry on their deceased husband's line. The only problem is that redeeming Ruth came with a high price. It meant putting his own estate at risk for Ruth's deceased husband. No one was willing to do that except Boaz. He risked everything to not just redeem Ruth, but to preserve the family lines of the husbands of both Naomi and Ruth. Their entire lineage was transformed because Ruth wasn't afraid to stumble into the unknown, stumble in another man's field as a lowly laborer, and stumble into the future with Boaz. And while her steps were not culturally and socially accepted, this Moabite woman's name stumbles into the genealogy of Jesus. (See Matthew 1:5.) That is a paradox of grace that can only happen when God breaks the rules to change the story.

Your story may not be one that has steady and sure steps, but when you allow God to use your life to show off His paradox of grace, you always end up falling forward instead of backward.

When you allow God to use your life
to show off His paradox of grace,
you always end up falling
forward instead of backward.

STRENGTH IN THE STUMBLE

The power residing in a stumble is a truth that is hard to accept. Most of us don't like the idea of stumbling because it denotes failure, struggle, and weakness. We'd rather be seen as strong, secure, and confident. God, however, would rather that we stumble with Him than walk secure in ourselves. We do our best to plan, prepare, and perform for the best possible outcome, but the reality is that sometimes things don't go as planned. That doesn't mean you've stumbled *off* the right path. It usually means you've stumbled off your own path and stumbled onto God's.

Trusting God to set out a path for you and determining to walk it out always requires a dependency on Him that will conflict with your inner self-confidence and strength. It's a crossroads of faith that leads you not where you can go on your own, but where you can go only with Him. And at that intersection of self-reliance and faith comes a stumble in our humanity that pleases God. A stumble from a heart that's been broken, but chooses to love forward again. A stumble that's birthed from the pain of living out of a hope that's been disappointed before, yet chooses to look to the future in faith. A stumble from a soul that's known the depth of loss too great to comprehend, but chooses to breathe in new life again for the future. Like in Ruth's story, the beauty of a stumble is the destiny it unlocks.

The beauty of a stumble is the destiny it unlocks.

The common misconception of stumbling is that you only stumble when you're doing the wrong thing. But sometimes we stumble merely from a weariness and exhaustion that God then uses to bring us into new strength we never knew we had. As we cope with the pressures and demands of life, it's easy to allow the fatigue and weight of our journey to bring us to a halt instead of causing us to stumble forward. I've seen too many people stop because they're worn out when they didn't realize holding on would have given them access to new strength. Think of a mother in labor ready to push her baby into the world. Though she's exhausted from enduring hours of labor, stopping is not an option. She must dig deep within and tap into a newfound strength until she hears the cries of her newly birthed baby. She may be stumbling under the pain and stumbling under the fatigue, but she's stumbling forward toward the promise of new life.

Strength found in your stumble is a strength unlike any other. It isn't progressive or gradual. It's the kind of strength that envelops you and launches you further than logic or reason can comprehend. It's the kind of strength that lets you stumble over the comments, criticisms, and negative views of other people. It's the kind of strength that breaks the rules of pain, opposition, and loss by giving you what you need to keep going when all you want to do is stop. It's the kind of strength that the prophet Isaiah wrote about:

Even youths grow weary and tired, and vigorous young men stumble badly, but those who wait for the LORD *[who expect, look for, and hope in Him] will gain new strength and renew their power; they will lift up their wings [and rise up close to God] like eagles [rising toward the sun]; they will run and not become weary, they will walk and not grow tired.*

(Isaiah 40:30–31 AMP)

And all the while, those who have banked on your fall, your demise, and your failure will be left stumbling in confusion, trying to understand how you found the strength to fall forward. God will make those whom you have stumbled in front of begin to stumble over you because your story is breaking their rules. They thought you were going to lay down and die. They thought you were going to pass out, fade out, and lose out, but God had a plan all along to use that tiredness to bring you close to Him and show the doubters His strength.

CONFIDENCE IN THE FUTURE

Strength isn't the only part of God's paradoxical plan that comes from your stumble. Newfound strength will pick you up in your stumble, but newfound *confidence* in His protection will steady your steps as you move forward. Confidence in God's protection gives you the bold assurance that no matter how many times you stumble, you can never stumble out of His grace. When you live without confidence in God's protection, it's easy to assume your stumble is proof God has abandoned you in anger. This couldn't be further from the truth. Biblically, God has commanded a protection plan over your life to watch over the moments when you think you're destined to fall. He's so committed to your season of struggle and stumbling that Scripture tells us He has contracted angels to catch you from falling:

You can never stumble out of His grace.

Because GOD'*s your refuge...evil can't get close to you, harm can't get through the door. He ordered His angels to guard you wherever you go. If you stumble, they'll catch you; their job is to keep you from falling.*
(Psalm 91:9–12 MSG)

The Hebrew context indicates the angels will keep you from falling away—falling away from God, falling away from your destiny, and falling away from the faith to believe you'll get back up again. If God would send an "angel" named Boaz to Ruth, I know God will send an angel to you to keep you from falling. Come on, somebody!

You may fall, but you'll always fall forward and you'll never fall alone.

One of the greatest joys of being a grandparent is being able to pass on certain traditions to my grandkids. Gracin is five years old and he's a stud. One day Gracin came to me and said, "Grandpa G, I need to ride a bike like JJ." Now JJ is his stud older brother and, needless to say, JJ does not have training wheels on his bike. Gracin was ready to ride with the big boys and I was more than happy to help. I taught his mother, Carissa, to ride a bike and it was nostalgic to now be able to teach her son as well. I got Gracin on his bike without training wheels no problem. The problem was keeping him off the ground. For the first couple of attempts, I held on as his anchor so he didn't tip too much to one side and fall off. After a while I started letting go and running alongside him, ready to catch him if he started to fall. He would lean to the left and then lean to the right trying to get into a rhythm of balance while I chased him from behind just in case I needed to step in to catch his falling. As I ran over and over again at his side, cheering him on with the California sun lighting our way, I could see his confidence get stronger and stronger with each lap. It's not that he thought he wasn't going to fall; it's that he knew I would be right there to catch him.

God and His angels are doing the same thing right now in your life. They're running alongside of you, cheering you on, ready to step in and catch you if lose your balance. You may fall, but you'll always fall forward and you'll never fall alone.

With an assurance like that, we can live knowing that if we do lose our step, help is close behind. Just imagine if we really lived with a confidence in God's protection. What if we genuinely believed every step was a step in the right direction, no matter how out of step it might seem? Would we handle our mistakes, fears, and slip-ups differently? Would we stop beating ourselves up with a list of should've-could've-would'ves? Your life may be filled with ups and downs, but it's never without His hand of protection. When you come to the realization His protection is not only for your provision, but also for your power, you'll approach each step in your life with a new confidence.

NO ONE ESCAPES THE PROCESS

The process of falling forward into new strength and confidence is most likely not a new process to you. Most of the breakthroughs in our life didn't happen because they were planned. They happened because we stumbled into them. This is the theology of stumbling that we must humbly learn as we let God break our rules. I'm not sure how many times you've stumbled this week, this month, or this year, but I can tell you every one of those stumbles will yield strength and confidence in you if you let it.

Once we stop seeing *stumble* as a bad thing, we can begin to see it the way God sees it. We can begin to see it as a necessity to our destiny instead of a detriment to our development. The paradox, or irony, in the theology of stumbling is that we can't get to strength without weaknesses. An addict can't break free until they've fought through their weakness for a certain substance or thing. An athlete can't break their personal record until they've battled out their plateau. An executive can't break through their mediocrity until they've contended with their competencies.

It's not too late to look back on your journey through life and start today to carry a different perspective about your steps. Right now, you can choose to stop excusing, fighting, and hiding your stumble and instead begin to see the footprints of your destiny.

No matter how privileged, how pristine, or how perfect a person may seem, they still cannot escape the process of stumbling into promotion. No one escapes the process.

> # No matter how privileged, how pristine, or how perfect a person may seem, they still cannot escape the process of stumbling into promotion.

David quickly came to understand the process of promotion. He experienced first-hand the ups and downs that came with it. After his victory over Goliath, David was despised and hunted by a jealous King Saul. Thinking he has no option but to flee, David goes to the one place no one could have ever expected: he goes to the Philistines. The very enemy he defeated now becomes his refuge. Here's David, who just killed Israel's greatest enemy, being adored and praised by the people he will one day lead, but instead of celebrating, he's running into the enemy's camp out of fear. He goes from killing an enemy to living with his enemy. Saul alone was not enough to drive David to such an extreme. It was hopelessness, fear, and desperation that proved to be greater enemies to David than Saul. He's broken, bruised, and beaten, but God has not forgotten him.

God allows David to live in the Philistine camp for over a year and even allows him to walk in favor and gain the city of Ziklag as his own. God breaks His own rules to protect and favor David through the hands of his enemies, even when David no longer honors God. The fact that God stays more committed to David's future in his moment of stumbling than to God's own rules tells us that God can be trusted in all of our wandering and stumbling. Tired from warring, David and his men stumble back home to

Ziklag to find their homes burned, their wives taken, and their possessions stolen. (See 1 Samuel 30.) The Bible tells us that these men wept until they couldn't weep anymore. They may have been warriors on the battlefield, but loss on their home field was enough for them to lose every ounce of courage and strength. David stumbles back to God and asks Him for direction on what to do next. For the first time in a long time, David stumbles out of his own choices and makes his way back to God's choices.

David probably thought God was going to tell him to accept his losses since it was his own choices that had brought on this heartbreak. But God's response is the exact opposite:

> *David inquired of the LORD, saying, "Shall I pursue this troop? Shall I overtake them?" And He answered him, "Pursue, for you shall surely overtake them and without fail recover all."* (1 Samuel 30:8 NKJV)

Let me clearly paint the picture of what God is telling David to do. He is telling David to go pursue, overtake, and recover all that he had acquired during his time living in the enemy's camp. God wants him to go after what he attained in the wrong place, in the wrong way, and by the wrong methods. Now, God could have easily given David everything he lost and more if He wanted, so why would God want him to recover Ziklag, a Philistine city? Maybe it was because God was more concerned about David stumbling back into trusting Him than about punishing him. Maybe it was because God wanted David to know without a shadow of a doubt that He was with him in his stumbling just as He was with him when He first called him from the field. Maybe it was because God wanted David to see that he could pursue, overtake, and recover his destiny just like he was about to pursue, overtake, and recover his possessions.

David needed Ziklag because Ziklag pulled the king out of David—though it didn't look like it at the time. How many times have we found ourselves stumbling into places we never dreamed we'd be and still God finds us? How many times have we tried to stumble out of our own destiny because we're too discouraged to go forward, and still God holds on to us? How many times have we tried to hide from God's call only to end up stumbling back into God's arms again? God will break any rule that stands in the way of getting you back to the right place.

God has designed our stumbling-places to confirm His identity in us. Your stumble will always give you a chance to get back up, set things right, and restore what's been lost. It's a guarantee that who He has called us to be is weaving its way into our hearts to produce a character that's broad enough, deep enough, and wide enough to fall forward into our destiny. That moment in Ziklag was God's way of protecting his anointing and call, not only then, but also for the years to come when David would need to come back to confession for restoration. God will always give you placeholders in your life to remind you how to get back up when you find yourself stumbling in the future. He pays it forward to show you that if He can keep you falling forward now, He can keep you falling forward in the future.

WHEN YOU STUMBLE INTO YOUR DESTINY

Jessica was nine years old when she stumbled into an unimaginable pain worse than what any child should ever have to bear. She came from a single-parent home with a mother who wanted to remarry for her children's sake. Never imagining the man she chose would harm her daughter, Jessica's mom welcomed Jim into her family in hopes of starting a future together. A few months later, the abuse started and Jessica became the victim of her step-father's attention in ways that left her crippled with helplessness and fear. Wanting desperately to be a good girl, she quietly hid the abuse and braced herself every night for the darkest pain she'd ever known. When he left her bedroom, Jessica would silently cry herself to sleep and pretend it was all a nightmare that she would one day wake up from. Every morning for over three years, she would convince herself that the night before hadn't been real.

Worse, even though her brother slept in the same room, they never spoke about what happened at night out of shame and fear. Some days she stumbled into denial while other days she stumbled into anger. As the nights of torment continued over the years, she fell deeper and deeper into depression, believing that everyone in her house knew about the abuse, including her mom, but did nothing to help her. She told herself over and over again that if someone was going to save her, it would have happened by now.

One day at school, she sat in an assembly about sexual abuse and watched as puppets acted out the secret life she had been suffering through. For the first time in three years, she realized she had to try to speak out. In her aching to be free, she had stumbled on a strength that had no business in the heart and mind of a young twelve-year-old girl. At home she told her mom about the assembly, and it was in that brief moment of honesty that her mother truly saw how much Jessica had changed. She gently asked Jessica if anything like what she saw at school had ever happened to her, and quietly Jessica began to cry. Unable to say his name out of fear and shame, she could only scrawl the three letters that opened up a floodgate of agony silenced for years: J-i-m.

In an instant he was out of the home, but not out of Jessica's memory. Lost in her own grief, Jessica's mother never spoke to her about it in the years that followed. The details, the rage, and the brokenness remained caged in Jessica's heart as she stumbled into adulthood. One Sunday morning, Jessica found herself in a service that introduced her to Jesus. Carrying all the years of shame to the altar, she gave her life to Christ and began to fall forward into a destiny that surpassed her past. She forgave, she healed, and she stumbled into a woman who was no longer a victim. She became a beautiful example of a turned heart, and she never looked back at the pain she had endured as a young girl.

Twenty years later Jessica sat on her couch facing her son in disbelief. Through tears of shock, she absorbed the blow of truth that her son had been molested by a teacher at school for over a year. How could she have missed it? How could she have failed him the way her mother had failed her? Stumbling over words and emotions too great to articulate, she found herself pulling from the same place of strength and healing that had guided her forward before. She vowed to do things differently than her own mother had. She swore to herself that they would talk about the abuse as a family, get justice as a family like she had never had, and heal together as a family.

She let God break the rules inside her heart that argued this shouldn't have happened again. She let Him take her back to the pain of her own abuse to pull her own son out of his. She allowed Him to break her family's heart to rebuild a stronger, more unified family. She let Him work through the paradox of pain to produce a destiny in her, in her son, and in her family that caused them to trustingly fall forward in Him.

A LIBRARY OF GOD'S GRACE

Stories like Jessica's are brutal to us, but beautiful to God. Stories like this break our rules on how God rescues, restores, redeems. They're filled with more pain than we're comfortable acknowledging and covered in more grace than we can comprehend. They're the stories of a generation that God is raising who know Him as the God who walks with them in their struggles and isn't silent in their stumbles. They are the great tales of a redemption that lead us to face our stumble headfirst and heart-first, not find a way around it. These are the stories that change the rules of *who* God can use and *how* He can use them. These are your stories, my stories, and the stories of those yet to be born. These are the stories of a paradoxical God who breaks our rules to pen a greater ending than we could have ever dreamed of.

The church should be a library of stories like these. There should be Ruths, Davids, and Jessicas in every church because this is the church God is raising. It's a church that has embraced the theology of stumbling to celebrate the most imperfect people, not the most popular. Churches who follow the paradoxes of God look for the ones who are struggling the most, not the least. I genuinely believe if we will embrace God's perspective on stumbling, we'll see more people stumble back to God to let Him rewrite their story.

What story is God trying to write in your life right now? What have you been too afraid to stumble toward? What weaknesses and fears have you hid from Him that He has been trying to uncover? Your stumble is the story God is writing so that your life will overflow with the hope and faith that this is your last stumble. Not so that you can achieve perfection, but so that you would have the strength, confidence, identity, and grace to stumble into new areas with God. Your stumble hasn't disqualified you; it's actually qualified you. Your struggle hasn't frustrated God; it's actually attracted His favor. Your fall hasn't taken you backward; it's actually launched you forward into your destiny.

It's not too late to look back on your life and start to carry a different perspective about your steps. Instead of viewing your struggles as graveyards, see them as stumbles toward something better. You don't know who you truly are on the inside until you start allowing your struggle to lead you to your stumble. If you embrace the struggle you have been avoiding, you'll give yourself permission to embrace the new position God is calling you to. The new position at work, the new position in your relationship, the new position at school are all the direct result of letting your stumble shape you from the inside. It's time to make a decision to no longer stay back as a harvester of the field when God is promoting you to something greater.

Today, make a decision to not just run across the finish line of this chapter in your story. Choose to lean in, head-first and heart-first, even if that means risking stumbling publicly. For some of you, this means forgiving the unforgivable. For others, it means reaching out toward a dream you thought you let go of years ago. And for still others, this means letting go of every inner argument, excuse, and defense and truly believing your imperfections have gotten God's attention. He's ready to risk it all to redeem you, publicly favor you, and bring you into His family lineage. All you have to do is start taking one stumbling step in front of the other while you keep your eyes on His promise in front of you. You have nothing to lose except all the things like doubt, fear, and guilt that have no place in your next chapter anyway. Your stumble is what leads you to Him.

So take a deep breath, close your eyes, and let yourself fall forward into His destiny. *It's time.*

The most foolish path is also the wisest one.

9

PUSHING BOUNDARIES

"We are limited but we can push back the borders of our limitations."
—Stephen Covey

I've always been the type of person who pushes the limits of what can be done; it's just part of who I am. As a kid, I pushed the boundaries of skateboarding both physically and culturally. Think a small, lanky Hispanic kid in skate park filled with predominately Caucasian kids twice my size and you'll get a pretty good picture of how I spent every weekend growing up in Santa Barbara, California. As a teenager, I pushed the boundaries of entrepreneurial success as the highest paid deejay in the city by the time I hit seventeen. After turning my heart to Christ, I pushed the boundaries of evangelism by radically preaching salvation outside parties and clubs. As a young pastor starting a church, I pushed the boundaries of ministry to raise a leadership team that was 75 percent unchurched and newly saved. They didn't qualify by the doctrines and standards of ministry, but an anthem of grace rose in our church through their lives that still echoes in the dream team that is building Cornerstone's next chapters.

The one common denominator in every season of my life has been *favor*.

FAVOR AND OBEDIENCE

Favor is the ultimate boundary-pusher. Favor will take you where you have no business being. It will shift conversations in your direction by bringing your name to a table that didn't originally have a seat for you. It will bring you among the great as evidence of how God perceives you while others who doubted you are left only to watch. Relationships, promotions, and doors of opportunity will open themselves to you even though you didn't push. What was once difficult for you to fathom or accept will now be possible for you to achieve. Favor is the one component in life that can make all the difference.

Your future is connected to favor, and favor is closely connected to your obedience. It's your willingness to follow after a God who isn't confined by the rulebooks of religion that moves you to the front of the line of favor and gives way to possibilities that were once too far out of reach.

Your future is connected to favor, and favor is closely connected to your obedience.

You might be thinking, *If God is the God who breaks rules, why would obedience be the key to unlocking favor?* It's true that the favor of God, like His grace, is a paradox that doesn't make sense to us because it's not dependent on us. It's part of who He is, not part of who we are. We can't give it and we can't take it away, but we can receive it. It's based on His position, not ours, and it only adds to the paradox that God would share His privileged position with us. His favor separates us from the world and marks us as His. Most of us have lived so long without the favor of God that we can't always recognize it at work on our lives. God wants to push your boundaries far enough out that you can believe once again that God can and will favor you. This faith to believe in God's favor sets you up to believe in a future that is unrestricted, unlimited, and unhindered by rules.

Now that rules no longer stand between you and Him, we must remember God doesn't want disobedience; He just wants an obedience to Him. What exactly does He want you to obey? He wants you to obey the ridiculous commands that don't make sense to you but make sense to Him. It's the type of obedience that Jesus talked about in the book of John:

> [Jesus said,] *"Those who accept my commandments and obey them are the ones who love me. And because they love me, my Father will love them. And I will love them and reveal myself to each of them."*
>
> (John 14:21)

This Scripture teaches us that when we have a relationship birthed from a genuine love and desire to know Him, serve Him, and follow Him, we will accept His commands and *want* to obey them. There is a covenant of relationship, not rules, that gives way to a covenant of obedience. And from that covenant comes a well of favor, rich with His unconditional love, grace, and personal revelation to your life.

A life that begins to become a reality when we come face-to-face with a ridiculous command from God.

DAVID'S RIDICULOUS OBEDIENCE

The irony about a ridiculous command from God is that it will usually seem like the exact opposite of what we "should" do. When we've been wronged, our natural response is to retaliate, but God's ridiculous command is to forgive entirely. When we've lost deeply, it makes sense that we'd pull back for fear of enduring loss again, but God's ridiculous command is to push forward. When we've gained something, our initial response is to hold on tight to preserve it, but God's ridiculous command is to give it away. These commands give us a revelation that God's methods are often radically different from ours. It's not going to make sense to us because we don't see the way our story ends. All we see is an *ask* of faith from God that puts us at a crossroads between what is logical and illogical. Yet however ridiculous it seems, we must obey.

David found himself faced with a ridiculous command that pushed the boundaries of his loyalty to God and his loyalty to his king. Saul had a love/hate relationship with David that vacillated from calling David his son to chasing him down to kill him. David ends up fleeing from Saul all over the country until he just so happened to have the opportunity of a lifetime to go from hunted to hunter. In 1 Samuel 24, we find David and his men hiding in a cave when Saul unexpectedly enters the very same cave. David is close enough to stab him and end his hunted existence. Prompted by his men, David creeps close enough to Saul to kill him, but, at the last second, he chooses to cut the hem of Saul's robe instead, to humiliate him. In that time, touching a person's robe was like touching the person themselves. David's choice to cut Saul's robe was an assertion of his ability to take the throne by force. It was a brazen move that left David riddled with guilt and remorse.

Why does David immediately feel convicted instead of vindicated and justified? I believe it's because in that moment, David felt the sting of obeying the command of his men rather than the command of God. He had wavered out of the character of a king and into the character of the men he was called to lead. They wanted to kill Saul; David didn't. They wanted revenge; David didn't. They wanted to promote David before it was time; David didn't. Yet, David's actions show us that in an impulsive instant, he had taken on their cause instead of upholding God's.

David's weaknesses are clearly visible to God and to those around him, and he has the choice to humble himself and go back to his identity of a king or prolong the process of promotion. I imagine in that moment angels began to talk to David and remind him of who he was. In my holy imagination, I see their voices beginning to rise above the voices of David's men, which were so persistent in wanting to take advantage of this opportunity. I see them surrounding David and reminding him that there's still a king inside of him if he will do the ridiculous instead of the expected.

God's ridiculous command was for David to publicly confess his sin to Saul and declare that he would not join in Saul's fight. It wouldn't have made sense to his followers to honor a man who wants to kill him, but David obeys. He cries out to Saul and confesses his sin, bringing honor back to the throne that God is calling him to. The beautiful part about David's obedience to God's ridiculous command is that Saul sees the king in David because of his confession. Had David not obeyed God, Saul would not have said these words: *"And now I realize that you are surely going to be king, and that the kingdom of Israel will flourish under your rule"* (1 Samuel 24:20).

God will always use a ridiculous command to push you beyond your own boundaries. David's sin in cutting Saul's robe pushed his boundaries in while his obedience to God pushed his boundaries out. By obeying God, the throne is brought closer within David's reach.

TAKING THE NEXT STEP, THEN THE NEXT

When I obeyed God's ridiculous command to write my first book, *The Heart Revolution*, I had no idea what it would birth in my future. The only thing I heard from God was a command to write. For some of you, writing a book wouldn't be so ridiculous, but for me it was beyond ridiculous. I had never written anything resembling a book before in my life and the boundaries of my education were enough to keep the pen out of my hand. I didn't attend a prestigious school, nor did I have any published theses with my name credited, but I had a command. The process pushed my boundaries in ways that nothing ever had before and led me into the unknown. It was in the unknown that God entrusted to me again His dream to raise a generation to live, love, and lead from their hearts.

I knew where God wanted me to go but I had no idea what beginning steps I would need to take. Once I agreed to do what God commanded, God showed me I needed to surrender my heart to Him again. Not because my heart wasn't surrendered, but because my future needed a greater surrender. It was a surrender that exchanged my heart for His dream. And what I rediscovered was that His dream is always bigger than my dream. Immediately the boundaries of my life extended to be able to encompass God's dream and I started to see ridiculous commands from my past begin to make sense. Ridiculous commands from God, such as reading every different Bible translation I could find when I first got saved, keeping countless journals filled cover to cover with dreams since I was a kid, and immersing myself in books that I didn't even fully understand the first time I read them as a young teenager. God had been writing a book though my life since before I could even recognize His voice. All of a sudden, the next chapters of my life, once above and beyond, were now within reach.

I remember standing in my office with Georgina, holding up the first hardback copy of *The Heart Revolution*. It was surreal. In my hand was the manifestation of a ridiculous command come to pass, while in my heart was a ridiculous vision that I now needed to live out with a new passion. In an instant, I saw God's hand of favor begin to open doors that would amplify His message to the world. When I first started writing, my vision wasn't large enough, but by the time I had it in my hand I could see more of His vision for my future. There were times when I wanted to quit and live in a smaller future, but God wouldn't let me. He kept reminding me of that moment when I touched my future for the first time. It was a chapter in my personal story that led me to want to obey the next ridiculous command, and then the next, and then the next. Once I saw another sample of my future in Him, it was easier to see the promise.

It's not in the known that we discover
God's plan of paradox; it's in the unknown.

Living from God's dream pushes us to enlarge our vision, not only for what is possible now, but for what is possible even after the impossible becomes possible. Most of us dream of liberation from the rules and regulations that fence us in, but few of us have a dream beyond the dream of liberation. Such was the situation with the children of Israel in the book of Exodus. Their dream only included liberation from Egypt. When they got to the Promised Land, they didn't have a dream large enough to know how to live in it. With a limited dream and vision, they struggled to believe God and trust Him enough to venture into the unknown. And just like the children of Israel, if we don't push out boundaries to include more than liberation, what should take us eleven days will end up taking us forty years.

On the other hand, when you push beyond your boundaries and align your steps with the heart of God, He will break the rules to accelerate blessings in your life. During challenging seasons that test us spiritually, emotionally, and relationally, it's easy to want to step back instead stepping forward. We all want to know what's next, but if we know every step that comes next, we will live from a limited dream and limited faith. It's not in the known that we discover God's plan of paradox; it's in the unknown. And it's only when we push the boundaries of faith and logic that we begin to step into the unknown.

Think of it this way. If we were to take a blank piece of paper and draw a dot representing where we are and another dot representing where God is leading you, the empty space between those two dots would be the unknown. In that empty space, God begins to write things into your future that are beyond your reach if you stay planted at your dot. It's in the empty space in our life that God talks to us in ways that we've never heard before. When the money's in the bank, we don't need God to talk to us. When our marriage and kids are on the right track, we don't need God to talk to us. When everything makes sense, we don't need God to talk. But in the empty spaces where there is nothing known or seen between our dot and God's dot, we desperately need God to speak. Life's most painful circumstances form deep-seated beliefs that need a bigger God to dispel them.

It's not in the heart of God to leave you where He finds you. It is His will and good pleasure to push you out of complacency, not because He doesn't see your problems, but because He sees your potential. He knows that your future position will force you to deal with your present condition. Repeatedly, history has shown us that change never comes at the hands of the comfortable. Sometimes when we've been hurt, we begin to believe God will only grant us access to things within our reach and nothing more. But the Bible teaches us a radically different approach. Jeremiah says it this way:

Call to Me and I will answer you, and tell you [and even show you] great and mighty things, [things which have been confined and hidden], which you do not know and understand and cannot distinguish.

(Jeremiah 33:3 AMP)

When you call out to God with a relentless pursuit to believe beyond the rules and regulations, God will give you an ambition to reach for things in Him that were once hidden and out of your reach. The purity and holiness of your desire to serve Him and glorify Him because of relationship, not religion, extends your reach further than ever before. Even into places you haven't reached for a long time.

RIDICULOUS COMMANDS GET PERSONAL

Paul and Linda had been married for almost thirty years when Linda called me up. They wouldn't say *happily* married because they weren't. They lived under the same roof, but existed in two completely separate worlds. They existed as Mr. and Mrs. on paper only. She was cold and silent while he was brash and callous. He was her provider and she was his caregiver. She was a shadow of the woman he once married and he was a silhouette of the man she once loved. They had no children and walked through the years of their marriage together at first, but with each passing day, slowly retreating more and more to their own corners. Her boundary line was when he started talking about money and their constant need for more of it. His boundary was when she shut down and stared at him with lifeless eyes. Every day their lines moved further and further away from each other and their future seemed lonelier and lonelier.

It was the perfect condition for God to step in and ask them to do the ridiculous.

Our church was doing a series called "Taking the Limits Off of God!" when I got Linda's email. It was polite, respectful, and angry. She voiced her frustration at my latest sermon that challenged couples to do one thing for each other that week that they used to do but had stopped doing. She wanted to know if Paul had shared with me their last disagreement and asked me to talk to her through my sermon from the pulpit. Apparently, their last argument almost exactly mirrored what we had discussed on Sunday. (Funny how God has a way of getting through to us when we've shut down every other line of communication!) She was quite upset that I had the nerve to air their dirty laundry in front of the whole church on a Sunday morning. She left a number, so I called her up to assure her I had not spoken to Paul and that, in fact, it was the Holy Spirit who had spoken to them in the service, not me. She didn't believe me initially but agreed to let her offense go.

Two weeks later, I got another email. It was even angrier than the first. Convinced I had again exposed their marital issues from the pulpit, Linda was livid at my audacity. Again, I called her and assured her I had no knowledge of their marital details. She still didn't believe me. Two more weeks went by and again I got another email. Determined not to be duped again, she would only agree to speak with me if her husband was present. I couldn't have agreed more. The following week we met and Paul vehemently denied sharing the details of their situation with me. Watching them sit in my office angry and frustrated, I asked them just one question: "Why is it so hard to believe that God would invade our service to talk directly to you about your marriage?"

Stunned by my question, they looked at each other and waited for the other to speak first. Finally, Paul cleared his throat and said, "Because, Pastor, God doesn't want anything to do with us." Now it was my turn to sit stunned. How could a couple who went to church every week believe God had written them off? While Linda sat quietly crying, Paul started to explain why they had ended up in this painful place as husband and wife. When they were dating, Linda had become pregnant and was too afraid to tell her devout parents. Without any support or confidants to share their sin, they decided to get an abortion before anyone could find out. The years passed and they were unable to conceive again. Each one blamed the other and they both silently blamed God. In their marriage, the lines had been drawn with permanent ink.

It took time for them to begin to trust me and my wife with the marker of their marriage, but we refused to give up. Slowly Georgina and I walked through the lines of anger, shame, regret, and loss, and each time we'd push back a barrier, we'd celebrate a small victory. We led them through every ridiculous command God wanted them to obey in order to bring the marriage of their dreams back within their reach. Commands like:

- Walk in forgiveness even if forgiveness is the last thing you want to do.

- Let the pain and anger of yesterday no longer have a place in your today.

+ Put the word *hope* back into your language.

+ Love each other as partners instead of hating each other for not being parents.

+ Give up the right to be right about all the wrong things.

Each command took on a life of its own that challenged them, broke down walls within them, and, as they allowed it, began to heal them. Some days we could see progress. Some days all we could see was setbacks. Some days were celebratory. Some days were not. Every day, God pushed through a boundary line in them about Him and each other. Their journey is far from over, but their war with one another is.

WHEN ABOVE AND BEYOND COMES WITHIN YOUR REACH

If I were to ask you what the one boundary is that's holding you back *right now*, what would you say? Is it fear? Intimidation? Insecurities? Guilt? Selfishness? What is the boundary line in your life that stops you from trusting in God's illogical plan? Chances are you already know the answer. What is it going to take to get you to see past your own boundary lines to start living the unrestricted life you were born to live?

On the other side of God's ridiculous commands is the marriage you've been praying for, the career you've been working so hard to achieve, the peace that you've been longing to experience, and the more that you haven't even begun to hope for yet. God wants to see if you want what He wants for you bad enough that you'll let Him lead you where you've never been before. Before we can see the breakthroughs in the unknown, we have to be willing to break through the knowns.

The unrestricted life found in God is radically different from the unrestricted life of man. The unrestricted life of man has one rule: me first. It is a life of unleashed pride, with every purpose, plan, and pleasure centered on one's self. The unrestricted life found in God, however, requires the humility to lay down the plans you carried for yourself for an even greater plan in Him. It requires our yes. When we say yes to letting God break our rules, we have no idea who will be the beneficiary. We can only see the grace for us to push past old boundaries to new journeys, but God sees the tens, hundreds, and thousands who have inherited grace through our unrestricted yes. The Bible says it this way, *"As grace is spread to the multitudes, there is a growing sound of thanks being uttered by those relishing in the glory of God"* (2 Corinthians 4:15 VOICE).

> ## The unrestricted life found in God requires the humility to lay down the plans you carried for yourself for an even greater plan in Him.

Your belief in an above-and-beyond God who isn't afraid to use grace and paradoxes to change the world triggers a contagious sound of gratitude from those following after you. It's a growing sound that is overthrowing the condemning voices of old rules, old plans, and old pains. Because we are willing to create room for God to extend our reach now instead of cluttering our hearts with laws and rules, we create room for others to reach even further in their relationship with Him.

Someone, somewhere, needs you to push out your belief boundaries to make room for them to believe. Your footsteps into the unknown create a pathway for your family, your friends, and your circles of influence to follow. Your faith in a new revelation of God gives those behind you a glimpse of a God who isn't restricted by religious boundaries. Your existence becomes proof that an above-and-beyond life isn't determined by the boundaries of sin. God can now use you to show the world the same God Jesus came to represent—not a God who is limiting and angry, but a God who is welcoming and forgiving. This is why God wrote this book and this is why He chose you.

Who is waiting for you to believe in the God who breaks the rules?

BEYOND LIMITATIONS

Unfortunately, even as God calls us upward and onward, our own nature tries to call us downward and backward. Our old nature wants to bind us to limiting boundaries, but God's nature in us and through us frees us to reflect our new revelation of Him. His nature of grace overshadows our old nature's judgement of itself and others. His nature of truth overpowers our old nature's self-deception. His nature of favor overcomes our old nature's passive acceptance of a marginalized future. His nature of inclusivity overthrows our old nature's isolation.

When Jesus died on the cross, He reached out with both hands to us so that you and I could also reach out with both hands for a new future with Him. He reached out with His right hand to cover all the wrong we'd ever do that would hinder us from getting right with Him. He reached out with His left hand to ensure we'd never get left behind. One hand wouldn't have been enough to silence our old nature, eradicate our old rules, and initiate a relationship with us that isn't defined by anything other than His love for us.

What if the only thing that stood between you and the life you were created to live was your willingness to obey His ridiculous commands?

Now it's our turn to reach out to Him with both hands. We reach out with our right hand to surrender our own righteousness in exchange for His. We reach out with our left hand to signify all that we've left behind to follow Him into the unknown. And in our reaching out, we find a hope and a future that is truly above and beyond anything we could have ever imagined. Allowing God to push our inner boundaries past what we've been, what we've known, and what we've done is how we move from discovering the God who breaks the rules to *obeying* the God who breaks the rules.

What if the only thing that stood between you and the life you were created to live was your willingness to obey His ridiculous commands? Would you obey what doesn't make sense if it meant seeing the unimaginable come to pass? Would you follow Him into the unknown if it meant knowing more about Him? Would you push the current boundaries in your life if it meant an unrestricted life with Him in the future?

Right now your present conditions may look like a far cry from an above-and-beyond life in Him, but that's just proof you're closer than you think.

God broke the rules when He sent His Son to push the boundaries of our relationship with Him and He is ready to do the same thing in your life. All you need to do is to trust Him, obey Him, and follow after Him. Every limitation in your line of sight is not a limitation to Him. If you will start today to look beyond your boundaries, you'll begin to see God break the rules and barriers that have kept you from stepping into the wide, open future He promised. When you see it, you can begin to walk toward it. And one step toward His ridiculous leads you one step closer to His miraculous.

Doing it again is the only way to do it for the first time.

10

THE POWER OF AGAIN

"Repetitio est mater studiorum."
Repetition is the mother of learning.
—Latin Proverb

Sometimes the ridiculous command from God is just one word—again.

The idea of repetition might emote feelings of dread as you think back to a grueling round of agains, like running windsprints or writing "I will not _____" five hundred times on a whiteboard. Or, it might bring a rush of adrenaline as you imagine replicating a previous success or achievement. Despite the contrary emotions associated with repetition, God wants us to bring a mastery to the word *again* to bring a *gain* in your life for the first time, the second time, or the hundredth time.

Anything you do again should bring a gain. If it doesn't, then it's time to do it again in a fresh new method. If it's working, then it's time to do it again with a fresh new vision.

The greatest obstacle to appreciating the power of *again* is the tendency to focus on the harvest, the result, instead of the focusing on the seed, the preparation. But a harvest doesn't produce a harvest; only seed can produce a harvest. Too many times, when we're asked to do something again and again, we only want the result and lose sight of the transformative necessity of repetition. We want to skip to the end instead of submitting ourselves to the process. But nowhere in life do we master anything unless we have done it over and over again.

Remember when you learned how to read? It wasn't until you kept repeating sounds and syllables that you learned how to open up the vast world of literature. Remember when you learned how to drive? You didn't get better on the road until you got behind the wheel over and over again. And remember when you learned to play an instrument or sport for the first time? It didn't feel like second nature to you until it became part of your nature through repetition.

WHEN GOD NEEDS YOU TO DO IT AGAIN

It's the same way with God. He doesn't become part of your everyday life, everyday thoughts, or everyday conversations until you make Him part of your every single day. I am not advocating an automatic, robotic repetition based on religious ideas of what's right and what's wrong. Instead, I want you to aim for a repetition that comes naturally out of relationship. And the difference between repetition from religion and repetition from relationship is the new posture of *revelation*.

God doesn't become part of
your everyday life, everyday thoughts,
or everyday conversations until you
make Him part of your every single day.

Without revelation, our repetition becomes just habitual, void of thought or intentionality. *With* revelation, our repetition become a gateway to genuine, consistent interaction with God that reflects an engaged, present, and involved parent. This was the relationship God always intended us to have with Him.

Instead of being synonymous with boring, monotonous, and tedious, God is breaking the rules to make the word *again* synonymous with *resilient*, *effectual*, and *prevailing*.

It's stepping up, stepping in, and stepping out every time as though it's the first time.

But what happens when you've been obeying God's ridiculous commands for a while and you start to feel like all you ever do is obey? It's human nature, when we lose our passion for something and are told we have to do it again, to begin to feel stifled by what once liberated us. We begin to see God as a rule-keeper again because we no longer want to stay in the longevity of pursuit after Him. No one wakes up one day and intentionally decides to rebel against a genuine relationship with God. It happens over time, small decision by small decision, to stop doing what we once did with vision and passion. When we let what we do *for* God become a habitual ritual, eventually what we do *with* God suffers and becomes a habitual ritual.

God is not a stagnant God who only reveals Himself once. He is constantly changing the dynamics and methods He uses to reach us—but if we become overfamiliar with Him, we won't be able to see Him shifting in our life. We can avoid that overfamiliarity by living out of *spiritual* repetition rather than *habitual* repetition. As I hinted at earlier, habitual repetition is repeating the outward manifestation of an action, but *spiritual* repetition is repeating the spirit, or heart, behind the action. The difference between the two is what makes or breaks a Christian over time. Each one of us will have to decide whether God is going to break the rules for us once or if He's going to be the God who *continues* breaking the rules for us over and over again. We can keep ourselves from putting Him in a box by confidently looking to Him for fresh new whys, new hows, and new whats. *Again* shouldn't just be about going through the motions. It's stepping up, stepping in, and stepping out every time as though it's the first time.

The beautiful thing is that mastering this paradox of fresh repetition will positively affect every other area of our lives as well. We will begin to stay in long-term pursuit in our marriages, parenting, education, leadership, ministry, and relationships with greater and greater insight and vigor as the years go by. In a culture where versatility is celebrated instead of longevity, endurance is in high demand. Our culture's incessant desire to always have options means that fewer and fewer people realize the benefit and value of doing the same thing consistently, and consistently well.

WHAT IF WE LIVED EVERY DAY LIKE MIRACLE JOY?

When my daughter Miracle Joy was young, we had a Friday tradition. We'd head over to a local restaurant that boasted all-you-can-eat pizza and ice cream and a fun room full of games and rides where you could work off the calories. After we ate, we'd grab our preloaded fun card and head over to our favorite game: the Big Bass Wheel. The Big Bass Wheel was a little over eight feet tall and weighed just over a thousand pounds. A worthy opponent for this father and daughter duo. Standing in the corner of the room, it called to us every week to step up, pull its handle, and spin the big wheel that protruded out of the bass's mouth to win various amounts of tickets. The majority of the spots on the wheel ranged from five to a hundred tickets, but the sweet spot was the Big Bass Bonus of a thousand tickets. Obviously MJ and I were always going for that ever-elusive perfect spin.

Every week we'd spin the wheel over and over again, racking up ticket after ticket. With each spin Miracle would look at me and say, "This is the one, Dad! Spin it again! We're getting a thousand tickets right now!" It amazed me that with every pull she never lost hope that that spin was "the one." Sometimes we hit the bonuses and sometimes we didn't, but Miracle would pull that handle again and again for hours with fresh hope, fresh expectancy, and fresh strength each time. There were times when I said, "OK, enough! We're done. Let's find another game to use our credits." But not MJ. She would keep pulling until every credit was gone and every spin was done. If she didn't hit the bonus before we left, she'd look at that Big Bass Wheel before we walked away and say, "Next week! Next week it's gonna to happen!"

I loved her tenacity in spinning it again and again even if it meant disappointment when the wheel stopped. As she got older, I watched the fruit of those long afternoons at the Big Bass Wheel. The way she approached each spin was the same way she approached everything in life: with perseverance, tenacity, and confident expectation.

What if we lived every day like Miracle Joy? What if we didn't let the last spin change our passion for the next spin? What if we didn't walk away and try something else when we hit a loss over and over again and chose instead to believe that the next time would be "the one"?

I know taking cues from a kid and her beloved fun room game is breaking the rules on how we adults learn, but maybe, just maybe, we can learn something from the Big Bass Wheel. Sometimes you're going to do something again and again and hit the jackpot. It's going to work out and you're going to feel rewarded for your persistence and determination. Other times you're going to do it over and over and over again and it won't work out. In those instances, you may feel cheated or taken advantage of because you didn't get to celebrate a win for the amount of credits you put in. You might feel like it was a waste of your time and investment and regret your *again*— but don't, because it wasn't. Your again is doing more in you and for you than what you can see. Your again is working out a reward that's far greater than what you want in that moment. Miracle Joy and I wanted the thousand tickets but what we walked away with was worth far more. Those times together won us a relationship filled with memories, laughter, and life lessons that we'll never forget.

When our life fluctuates and changes, we need to be able to look back at life lessons that we've learned along the way to get us through the next spin. Our core beliefs and principles help us make sense of the seasons that don't make sense to us. They lead us back to the God who pursues us, breaks rules for us, and calls us out to do it again and again.

DAVID'S TWO HABITS

I've often wondered why, in the fluctuating seasons of David's life, God continued to call him a man after His own heart. There were moments when David stood honorable and there were other moments when he was downright criminal! Why would God publicly compare Himself to David when David made distinct choices, decisions, and actions that were completely contrary to God's character?

Well, if we look at his life as a whole, there are two things David consistently did that led God to overlook the big rules David broke: he came back to worship and he came back to repentance—again and again. Those two postures made all the difference to God. Because He was able to clearly see the broken man in David, who so desperately wanted to do right when he did wrong, He was able to overlook the broken rules that David left behind. Those are the actions of a God who lives not in the realm of the comprehensible, but in the realm of the paradoxical. And in our life when our own choices, decisions, and actions often reflect the opposite of God's character, we need the same God to encounter our brokenness as well. When God sees the consistent places in your walk with Him, He will see past the inconsistencies and see you for who you truly are. David's inconsistent life may have brought consequences, but his relationship with God was never jeopardized. Even after his notorious affair with Bathsheba, when he not only took another man's wife but then killed the husband in order to cover up his adultery, God saw his willingness to repent and spared his life:

> Then David confessed to Nathan, "I have sinned against the LORD." Nathan replied, "Yes, but the LORD has forgiven you, and you won't die for this sin." (2 Samuel 12:13)

Why did God allow David to live? I believe we see the why just eleven verses later. God wasn't afraid to operate from the principle of *again* for David. After Bathsheba's first child dies, God gives David a second chance with another son named Solomon, whom He loved and favored. (See

2 Samuel 12:24.) Although David's actions grieved and angered Him, God favored him again because He would not go back on the vow He made to him before his fall with Bathsheba. God reminded David of all the times He had been with him because He knew David was going to need Him again.

> *This is what the LORD of Heaven's Armies has declared: I took you from tending sheep in the pasture and selected you to be the leader of my people Israel. I have been with you wherever you have gone, and I have destroyed all your enemies before your eyes. Now I will make your name as famous as anyone who has ever lived on the earth!* (2 Samuel 7:8–9)

It wasn't that God wanted to make David's name famous for David's own glory. No, God wanted David's name to be famous because, in the fabric of David's life, God had weaved a story of redemption, forgiveness, and favor, again and again. God used David's life to make His redemptive and favoring nature famous to us today. God knew we needed to know His heart to go after us again and again so we would go after Him again and again. In our rulebooks, there are limits to how often we forgive, but God has no such limits. He proves that over and over again throughout His Word and especially in the history of David the king.

In our rulebooks, there are limits to how often we forgive, but God has no such limits.

From this revelation of God's *again*, we find our own power to be sons and daughters who will make Him famous. Your *again* at work, at home, at school, and everywhere you go tells the world that you represent and follow an *again* God. And for a generation that has all too often only known betrayal, rejection, and loneliness, that exemplary faith speaks volumes. When we come to God and then walk away from Him out of offense, anger, or confusion and refuse to let Him to come after us *again*, we tell the world God isn't worth our *again*. But when we let the people in our world see that

God still forgives us when we aren't perfect, aren't consistent, and aren't right, we tell them that it's ok to come back to God again and again and again.

If our relationship with God looks like the corporate rat race after promotion and prestige, it's time for a fresh reality. If our relationships with each other look no different from the relationships of those who don't know Him, it's time for a fresh perspective. If the people in our world can't tell the difference between our faith and theirs, it's time for a fresh conviction. It's these new revelations that keep us from allowing our routines to ebb away our dreams. They protect us from getting lost in the things we need to do again and again. They hold us to a higher standard that yields a greater reward.

The world is a busy, hectic place and the need to slow down and focus on one thing and one thing only has never been greater. In a typical day, our phones don't stop ringing, our texts don't stop coming, and our meetings don't stop running into each other. Even when we go home at the end of the day, the multiple hats don't usually come off. The truth is we've lost the art of disconnecting from everything to be able to reconnect to one thing. Sometimes we need God to interrupt our incessantly busy lives to get us to focus on just one thing. Maybe that one thing is Him. Maybe that one thing is you. Maybe that one thing is your family. Maybe that one thing is the future. Whatever that one thing is, let it bring you back to a place where you can appreciate the *process* more than the *product*.

LESSONS FROM LANDSCAPING

Over the years, I've come to realize the most challenging people to inspire are those who have done things a certain way over and over again for years and not seen the fruit they expected. It's not that they're incapable of or against the new things God might be doing in their life. Rather, it's that they've experienced the highest level of disappointments and now they're scarred. When our lives are fruitful, it's easy to say we'll keep doing anything to keep yielding fruit. But when our lives are barren, it's even easier to want to walk away.

Let's look at a story Jesus told about a man who had experienced disappointment over and over again:

> *Jesus told this story: "A man planted a fig tree in his garden and came again and again to see if there was any fruit on it, but he was always disappointed. Finally, he said to his gardener, 'I've waited three years, and there hasn't been a single fig! Cut it down. It's just taking up space in the garden.' The gardener answered, 'Sir, give it one more chance. Leave it another year, and I'll give it special attention and plenty of fertilizer. If we get figs next year, fine. If not, then you can cut it down.'"*
> (Luke 13:6–9)

This parable hits pretty close to home for some of us. We've been the man who planted and planted but saw no fruit for years and years. We've felt the frustration of wanting to just cut something out of our life instead of trying to fix it again and again. But not all of us have heard the voice of God telling us to give it another chance. The reality is that this tree never gave any kind of fruit—not even one piece. It doesn't make sense why this gardener would ask for more time if he had never even seen a harvest. Most of us could understand fighting for something that gave at least some sort of indication that fruit was a possibility, but fighting to keep something that never had a return is illogical.

So what did the gardener know that his boss didn't?

My father taught me everything I know about life and landscaping. What I learned from him about each lent wisdom to the other and gave me knowledge and appreciation for the cycles and rhythms of growth. One piece of wisdom my dad always reminded me of was the process of maturation in trees and plants. When we would get a call from an upset client about a tree that wasn't producing what they expected, my dad would always say, "It's not ready. It's not mature yet. We'll keep taking care of it." Sometimes he would really get yelled at for trees that wouldn't produce at all and all he would say was, "You can't force it. It needs time." For some clients we'd have to go in and remove the trees because the clients just weren't willing to go through the process of waiting for it to mature. It wasn't until years later, when I was frustrated at things in my life that wouldn't produce what I expected, that

my dad told me the same thing he told his clients: "You can't force it. It needs time."

In the parable Jesus told, the gardener knew the value of time and patience in the maturation process. He understood that if he kept nurturing the tree, feeding it, and watering it again and again for another year, it would eventually bear fruit. Cutting it down would have revealed the immaturity of not only the tree, but also the man who didn't have the patience to give it more time to grow.

Sometimes God will withhold
a season of fruitfulness in our life
so He can expose the areas in us
that need to mature and grow.

Similarly, when we cut things out our life too soon instead of continuing to nurture them, feed them, and water them again and again, we expose our own areas of immaturity that need to develop. Sometimes God will withhold a season of fruitfulness in our life so He can expose the areas in us that need to mature and grow. While it may seem as though He's violating His own law of sowing and reaping by withholding a harvest, it is in actuality an indication of His authority over the harvest to determine its times and seasons. God wants us to desire the One in charge of the harvest more than desiring the harvest itself.

ONE COUPLE'S DARING "AGAIN"

Adam and Vanessa had been married for almost five years when they filed for divorce. They hadn't started out fighting but that's where they had ended up. They fought about money, careers, family, sex, the future, the past, and everything in between. They were tired of arguing every day and were ready to throw in the towel on the dreams of having kids, buying a home, and growing old together. It didn't seem worth it anymore when everything they tried failed over and over again. Even though divorce was never an option before they said "I do," it seemed to be their only option now. Too many bridges had been burned between them and too many words had been spoken in anger than could ever be forgiven. It was over—and as much as they both hated to admit it, they genuinely believed they were better off not married to each other. Even their families felt divorce was their best hope for finding someone better and trying again.

After the divorce papers were finalized, they each went their own way and kept no contact with each other. And for a period of time, they were better without each other. They pursued their individual dreams and were quite successful. They dated other people, but neither remarried for fear of going through yet another divorce. Both were in their early thirties and still felt they had plenty of time to find the right spouse. They were wrong. Not long after the ninth anniversary of their divorce, Vanessa was diagnosed with breast cancer. Devastated, she cried for weeks while her family and friends tried their best to remain hopeful. After three months of aggressive chemotherapy, Vanessa's results looked good and she tried to get back into what she humorously called her BC life—her "before cancer" life.

But Vanessa had changed. Cancer had made her different in a way that she couldn't explain. Wanting to make peace with God, she accepted an invitation from a coworker to check out one of our services. Vanessa walked into our church on a Sunday morning with her head down and her heart heavy. She wasn't sure what she was looking for, and she wasn't sure she wanted to be looked for either, but she was there nevertheless. At the end of the service she walked out and was just a few feet from her car when she heard her name being called. A little dazed and very confused, she turned around to see a familiar face coming toward her.

Adam wasn't sure how she'd react to seeing him, but when he saw her in the service, he knew he wanted to say hello. Thinner and frailer than he remembered, she hardly looked like the woman he argued with day and night almost ten years ago. He watched her for the majority of the service, wondering if he'd really muster up the nerve to say hello. At altar call, he tried to close his eyes, but couldn't help but open them every once in a while to see if she would raise her hand to accept Christ. Brushing tears from the corner of her eye, she had raised her hand but hadn't moved out of her seat to come to the altar. At the end of the service, she quietly gathered up her stuff and walked out, keeping her head to the ground the entire time. Adam tried to catch up to her and called out her name, but she didn't hear him. He felt like a fool and wanted to walk away, but somehow couldn't. He called out to her again just a few feet before she got to her car, and slowly she turned around.

They exchanged pleasantries and commented on how well they each looked while each awkwardly wondering what to do next. They spoke only for a few minutes, but it was a start. The following week Vanessa came back with the same heavy walk and head down. It took almost six months of occasionally bumping into each other before Adam had the courage to ask her to have coffee with him. She agreed but didn't know why. Over the course of the next year, Vanessa and Adam became friends again. They would sit together, attend life group together, and linger after service talking. Out of that friendship came a mutual regret for causing each other so much anguish when they were married. They recognized their mutual culpability for the divorce and expressed genuine remorse for how they had treated each other. They were different now, older and wiser, and their framework of life had changed since becoming Christians. Over and over again, they talked about how different their marriage would have been had they had a relationship with God back then.

The conversation about remarrying came up almost two years after they first saw each other outside our church. It seemed ridiculous, but still, it kept coming up. They joked about how funny it would be if they actually went through with it. It was Adam who realized they had been friends for longer since their re-acquaintance at church than they were while they were dating. When the cancer came back, Adam came back to the reality that God had given him another chance to grow old with Vanessa. Together they went through another round of chemotherapy and again talked about remarrying. On her last day of chemotherapy, Adam proposed again. They attended our marriage classes and said "I do" again in front of a group that was mixed with people who had been there for their first marriage and those who were ready to help them celebrate their second.

That year was the last time Vanessa's cancer came back, and it was the last year they spent a day apart.

SAYING YES AGAIN

There's a little bit of Adam and Vanessa in all of our stories. We've all walked away from something in our lives that we wish we could one day go back to. We've all walked through challenges that have made us rethink our relationship with God and eternity. We've all come to the place where our past catches up to our present and gives us a chance to rewrite our future. Adam and Vanessa chose to get married again despite the statistics that said they wouldn't make it. They chose to do it again when their family and friends warned them not to. They chose to do it again despite the fear that it would end up exactly the same as before.

I believe today is the last day you'll spend apart from God.

What would we choose if it was our story? Would we be able to give God another opportunity to do something new in our life? I would like to think we would—despite the risks, opposition, and fears.

What if God were to tell you that's exactly what He's doing through this book? What would you say if God told you He was using this book to bring you back to a place where you would be willing to renew your covenant with Him again? Would you be willing to let go of the old fights, arguments, and rules you had in your first relationship with Him? Would you let Him show you the *again* work He's done in healing you from all the pain and brokenness that threatened to kill you on the inside? Would you let Him bring people back into your life who've hurt you, disappointed you, and left you in the past?

I believe you're ready. I believe you'd say yes again. I believe this is the last time the cancer of rules will come back into your life. And I believe today is the last day you'll spend apart from God.

We are best served when we serve.

11

THE NOW AND THE NEXT

*"Great things in business are never done by one person.
They're done by a team of people."*
—Steve Jobs

Every system of rules must go through the process of progression to be able to reach a new generation. Think about how rules progressed in our own lives as we aged. When we were younger, the rules were pretty strict. But as we grew older, we found ourselves living with fewer and fewer rules and more and more freedom. It's not that the core principles behind the rules changed; it's that the methods have evolved.

Today, as the *now* generation and the *next* generation work side by side, the need to change our methods, not our core principles, is greater than ever. The need is great because the gap is wide. Never before has there been such an ideological gap as the one that exists today between the now and the next. The tired rules of yesterday have lost their luster and appeal to the next generation but the shifting rules of tomorrow offer little security to the now generation.

Rules are what has created this great divide. You see, rules don't just limit our relationship with God. They can also limit our relationship with others. They may start off with the right intentions, but if they become walls instead of bridges, they will inevitably only divide, alienate, and exclude.

Today, what one generation upholds as law is inconsequential to the other. What one generation includes, the other excludes. What one generation advocates for, the other fights to oppose. The rules that alienate the generations from each other begin as opinions—opinions that are unable to be broken, altered, or expanded. And an opinion that won't change becomes an inner rule that won't be broken. An opinion that won't adjust becomes an offense that won't forgive. An opinion that refuses the possibility of being wrong becomes a relationship that can't grow forward. When we forget that opinions can be purely subjective, we get stuck in our own ways and lose the ability to work together toward a common goal. And when we can't work together to achieve a common goal, the good that can be accomplished through the hands of many shrinks to fit into the hands of one. The Bible says it this way: "…one will put one thousand to flight, but two will put ten thousand to flight" (Leviticus 26:8; Deuteronomy 32:30 NKJV).

The widening generational gap is the fault of a mutual lack of agreement, honor, and respect that causes the war around us to become the war within us.

WHEN THE GAP WIDENS

The widening generational gap is not the fault of one generation or the other. It's a mutual lack of agreement, honor, and respect that causes the war around us to become the war within us. When the *now* sees the *next* getting favored through what they had to pay a high price for, the gap widens.

When the *next* sees the *now* imposing antiquated standards that are no longer relevant, the gap widens. When both the now and the next see the fruit of their labor being overpowered, overshadowed, and overlooked by the other, the gap widens.

No longer are our enemies only those who oppose our cause. No longer are our foes just those who rebel against God. No longer are our adversaries those who stand opposite kingdom beliefs and mindsets. Now, our enemies, foes, and adversaries are those who oppose us personally, rebel against us generationally, and stand opposite us philosophically.

And the wider the gap, the further God has to stretch to bring us back together.

A true inclusion of both generations means breaking down the barriers that hinder the strength of each generation. Each generation must be able to operate fully in honor, heart, and hunger. Honor from both the now and the next opens the gateway for legacy to be passed on and through to the next. Humility of heart in both generations insulates, protects, and averts relational repercussions. And hunger to see a greater demonstration of God's power and presence than any other previous generation drives them to work together instead of apart. When honor, humility, and hunger, all three, are alive and active in the next and now generation, there is a unified passion to stay loyal to the past while remaining ferociously committed to the future. And then there is no limit to what both can accomplish together.

Through the lens of rules, it would stand to reason one generation is right while the other must be wrong, but that's not always the case from God's vantage point. Through Jesus, God does not take a black-and-white perspective. God breaks the traditional rules of wrong or right to see the greater vision that gives up the right to be right for the right reasons. Sometimes the right reason is to bring peace in the midst of war. Sometimes the right reason is to attain a greater gain than loss. And sometimes the right reason is unknown until much later.

When David was anointed and called as next, Saul was still the now. God overlapped the now and the next for almost two decades before moving David into the kingship! Why did God promote David without first removing Saul? I believe God left Saul in David's life to deal with the "Saul" in David that had been birthed over the years of being formed under Saul's leadership. David had to see, and turn away from, the kind of influence and leadership that Saul exhibited. Sometimes God leaves now leaders in their position so that the next generation can see how not to lead. And, likewise, God left David in Saul's life to remind Saul that he, too, had been at one time chosen and called by God, just like David was, but that Saul had forgotten and rejected that call. It wasn't until many years after David was anointed as king that we see how God all along was dealing with both the David in Saul and the Saul in David.

The rules about rules need to change if the now and next generations are going to work in tandem to accomplish common goals. They may seem like two generations on opposite ends of the spectrum, but if we will allow God to build a bridge between them, we can begin to see a stronger future together. We can take the wisdom and experience of the now and merge it with the creativity and passion of the next to achieve a present-day power and strength that surpasses what one generation could accomplish on its own. Because God's plan for us is always far greater than we can comprehend on our own, it stands to reason that He would create a future for us that is also beyond our ability to achieve on our own. The now needs the next, and the next needs the now.

CROSSOVER LEADERSHIP

Often, the gap between the next and now generations is bridged by those who can speak to both. They facilitate the crossover leadership. They can be seen as the "middle" generation, and the Bible gives us a clear picture of their power and vital necessity in the book of Genesis.

When the patriarch Jacob was near the end of his life, blind and ailing, Joseph brought his two sons to him for a blessing. Now, Manasseh was the eldest grandson and represents the older, *now* generation of leadership. Traditionally, Jacob's right hand would rest upon Manasseh as a symbol of the greater blessing from God. Ephraim was the younger and represents the next generation of leaders. He would traditionally receive the left hand of lesser blessing.

They walked into the tent and Joseph positioned Manasseh at Jacob's right hand and Ephraim at his left. But then Jacob broke the rules and did something completely unexpected. He crossed his hands in the shape of an X, so that his right hand of power is on the younger son and his left hand is on the oldest son. Joseph thought his father had made a mistake, but Jacob knew exactly what he was doing:

> *Joseph was upset when he saw that his father placed his right hand on Ephraim's head. So Joseph lifted it to move it from Ephraim's head to Manasseh's head. "No, my father," he said. "This one is the firstborn. Put your right hand on his head." But his father refused. "I know, my son; I know," he replied. "Manasseh will also become a great people, but his younger brother will become even greater. And his descendants will become a multitude of nations."* (Genesis 48:17–19)

In our time, the "middle" generation could be thought of as Generation X, which, like Jacob, embodies the crossover conduit of blessing from the now generation, the Baby Boomers, and the next generation, the Millennials. Generation X carries the responsibility of bridging the transition of leadership to Millennials by releasing the right hand of power to the future while using their left hand to maintain an honor for the past. Because Generation X was led by the driving force of the Baby Boomers and is now being asked to lead with the sensitive touch of Millennials, they represent the opportunity to bring out the best of both generations. When Generation X leads Millennials to honor the past and the future, we see a collaboration that's stronger and wiser.

The transition between generations is also seen in Jesus' ministry. Most would argue that Jesus changed the world through the next generation as most of the disciples, it is believed, were younger than Jesus. This is true, but not entirely true. The disciples did not have the credibility to reach the world with Jesus' message of truth and grace. They lacked the experience, authority, and authenticity to radically revolutionize the world for Christ. To bridge the gap, Jesus knew He needed the *now* to stand beside the *next*.

Who were the now generation in the days of Jesus? It might surprise you, but it was the Pharisees. Through numerous biblical accounts, we know of Jesus' disdain for and condemning attitude toward the Pharisees so we naturally exclude them as part of Jesus' equation to change the world. However, if we look at Matthew 5, we read one line that gives us insight into how Jesus saw the Pharisees initially: *"For I say to you, that unless your righteousness exceeds the righteousness of the scribes and Pharisees, you will by no means enter the kingdom of heaven"* (Matthew 5:20 NKJV).

How could Jesus call them the standard of righteousness and then later call them a brood of vipers? Why would Jesus elevate them and then later denounce them? What changed?

The Pharisees were scholars of the law, living and operating under the only known revelation at the time. Jesus saw them as the now generation who could have helped the disciples fulfill the law the Pharisees knew better than anyone. He saw their potential to lead a generation that had both the knowledge of the law and the revelation of the Savior. What greater collaboration could there be?

The only problem is that the Pharisees didn't want to *just* be the now; they wanted to be the now who controlled the next. They wanted a Messiah who followed their laws and methods. They wanted the laws to remain as they understood them on their terms. Their love and knowledge of the law should have positioned them to be the now, but their refusal to be open to new methods and new revelation disqualified them. Their unrelenting rejection of Jesus's fulfillment of the law pushed Him to look for a new now. One that would be willing to break the man-made traditions of the law that hindered God's voice and limited His revelation.

So instead of calling the Pharisees to work alongside the disciples, God promoted the least likely guy in the world to represent the now—Paul, a murdering Pharisee whose real name was Saul. God throws out the rule book, intervenes in Saul's life on his way to murder more Christians, converts him, changes his name, and uses him to become the next now. (See Acts 9.)

It's an outrageous move on God's part, but Paul was perfect. He was older and wiser and more aware of the need to break the laws that prevented a genuine relationship with God. He brought to the table the ability to fully understand the law and fully understand the grace now written into the law by the blood of Jesus. He had legitimacy, authority, and one unbelievable story of conversion that no one could deny. He was the Generation X of his time, building the bridge that brought the now and next together.

But we can't forget that he wasn't who Jesus looked to first. Why is that important? Because if those of us who are the *now* lose sight of the need to constantly stay open to a greater revelation than we currently hold, God will have to find another, even if He has to break the rules to intervene. He'll find the Pauls who will be the bridge if He can't break down the Pharisaical walls within us.

Jesus represented a generation of leadership that was real, relevant, and radically new.

Jesus represented a generation of leadership that was real, relevant, and radically new. He was free from the religious bondage that plagued the Pharisees who despised Him. The Pharisees represented a generation of leadership that was rigid, stubborn, and hypocritical. However, just like every Pharisee wasn't like Saul (for example, Nicodemus) and every disciple wasn't like Jesus (for example, Judas), we have to remember that not everyone in the now generation leads like a Pharisee and not everyone is the next generation leads like Jesus. We must also remember that, on one level, generational gaps refer to age, but their roots really run much deeper than that. They are generally more reflective of a leadership model than of a certain age. If we can understand that the title of leader refers, not to the one in charge, but simply the one who went first, we will better understand the generational gap. A leader in the now can be spiritually older but physically younger than a leader in the next, and vice versa.

BREAKING THE RULES BETWEEN THE NOW AND THE NEXT

Before I started our church, I constantly fought to have both the now and the next beside me in order to reflect both the love for truth and the love for grace that came from the Spirit. But it wasn't until we opened up multiple campuses that I truly realized the depth of God's strategy for success in both the now and the next. When you're one campus, you can easily convey your mission and vision through the leaders beside you. However, when you multiply into other cities, communities, and countries, everything changes. I began to realize again how vital each generation was to the people God wanted to reach through our church. If you visit one campus, you might see the campus pastors there reflecting the now because that's the greatest need in the community they've been called for. Visit another campus and you'll see a campus pastor reflect the next because that's who they're reaching in their circle of influence.

What has made the difference has been each campus's ability to labor with now and next leaders beside them and raise now and next leaders behind them. They recognize they can't be both now and next in every season of their leadership, but they can produce fruit that reflects both the now and the next as a result of fighting to protect both generations. If our campuses only reflected one generation or the other, we wouldn't be able to fulfill the mission and vision God gave us and that would limit the generations to come after us.

Maybe you're not a pastor or leader who is building a multi-campus church. Maybe you're a business person who has the influence to reach the now world but you're not sure how to reach the next. Maybe you're a parent who is trying to figure out how to raise this next generation in a culture that's so different from what you grew up in. Or maybe you're a young person trying to figure out how to make your way to the next without a now mentor, leader, or pastor, beside you. Maybe your identity has always been in the next but God is moving you into the now, and you're stumbling into that new reality. Wherever you are in life at this moment—now or next—there are a few rules that need to be broken if we're going to bridge the gap between the now and next generations.

1. BREAK MISCONCEPTIONS AROUND TRANSITIONS

The first rule we need to break in bridging the generational gap are the misconceptions around transitions. We like to believe each generation is intended to hand off the reins to the one after it in perfect transition similar to a relay race. We love this analogy—until the hand-off gets messy. Some of us want to hand off our portion and slow to a stop while others want the hand-off to come sooner so that they can take off on their own race.

A closer look at this analogy can give us some needed perspective. In a relay race, there are a few things necessary for a transition. First, the receiving runner always starts running before the hand-off. Once they're off and running, the baton goes into their hand. It's never handed off in a resting position. Second, the receiving runner isn't looking backward for the baton. They keep their hand extended back and wait for it to be placed in their hand. It's the runner handing the baton off that has the job of putting it the right place. Third, the hand-off always changes hands from left hand to right hand or right hand to left hand. It's never the same hand that gives and receives.

If you're the next generation, are you ready to run without anything in your hand or are you waiting to possess it before you can run with it? If you know what's been promised to you by God, you can start running with your eyes focused ahead *as though* you already have it.

Nothing that is passed on
ever stays the same.
It's *supposed* to change.

If you're the now generation, are you running your race to hand off your baton and empower the next? The next generation must feel like everything from God's hand to yours is now being handed off to them as though it's God empowering them through you. Remember, it's the job of the *now* to make sure what's in their hand makes it into the hand of the *next* generation, not the other way around.

For both the now and the next generations, are you looking together for ways to switch hands for a new method? Nothing that is passed on ever stays the same. It's *supposed* to change. If we're going to see a radically different outcome in our now and next generations, every family, every business, and every church is going to need a hand-off strategy that prepares both generations for a greater victory at the finish line.

We can see how this happened at key hand-offs in the Bible. David was already running in the field when the baton hit his hand from the prophet Samuel. The disciples Simon Peter and Andrew were already running as fishermen when Jesus called them to be fishers of men. When Paul was given the baton, it switched from the left hand of power to a new right hand of authority and influence. It was the change of influence that was needed to remedy all the methods that weren't working when the Pharisees held the baton.

Every one of these hand-offs from the now to the next were messy but necessary. Some of them broke the rules to receive their batons and some broke the rules to hand them off, but if they hadn't, we wouldn't have an example to follow toward victory. When we work together, we will get better at transitions and hand-offs. We'll want to see one another give and receive everything God put into our hand in the best possible way so we can celebrate a joint triumph instead of an individual victory.

2. BREAK THE RULE OF INSTANTANEOUS TRANSFORMATION

The second rule that needs to be broken when we're working together as allies is the rule of instantaneous transformation. As technology has advanced and made almost everything virtually instantaneous, we tend to apply that same principle to every area of our life. Pop in life lessons on the car ride to school, and *poof!* a well-managed and well-prepared kid should jump out after school. Throw in some Scriptures on a Sunday morning and *voila!* a well-versed disciple should be ready by the end of service. As I'm sure you are thinking, it doesn't exactly work like that, even though sometimes we'd like it to. Transformation takes time.

Transforming the next generation to become the now generation will take time just like transforming the now generation to take backseat to the next is going to take time as well. When we force transitions too soon from either generation, we miss the opportunity to see genuine discipleship take place. We miss the conversations that bring us closer, the unspoken lessons that we learn by watching over time, and we miss the answers to questions we encounter along the way. Overnight success is not impossible, but overnight team success is. Teams need time, and time means slowing down to explain, listen, and adjust. If the now doesn't commit to building genuine relationships with the next, we inadvertently contribute to the abandonment of leadership by the next. Slowing down may frustrate you, but nothing is more frustrating than the right person pushed into the right position at the wrong time.

> Slowing down may frustrate you, but nothing is more frustrating than the right person pushed into the right position at the wrong time.

3. BREAK THE RULE OF NON-TRANSPARENCY

The third rule that's kept the now and the next stuck on opposite sides is the notion that each generation can't be transparent. There is an unspoken rule that keeps the now and the next from being transparent for fear of being perceived as weak and replaceable. It's this erroneous idea that has left the now and the next battling each other instead of battling together. Sharing our pain, our worries, and our weaknesses should be as natural to us as sharing our accomplishments, victories, and strengths. When parents, bosses, and leaders are transparent about their struggles, they unobtrusively give their children, employees, and disciples the right to also be human with real challenges. Trusting others to regard us in the same light, though we are not perfect at every given moment, allows us to relate with one another beyond titles, ambitions, and agendas. It's this philosophy that allows us to influence the next generation up close rather than simply impact them from afar. And likewise, when we create opportunities for either generation to get back up when they stumble, we create a stronger trust and faith in one another rather than tearing one another down.

WHEN THE NOW AND THE NEXT WORK TOGETHER

When my mother passed away unexpectedly just over a year after my father's passing, it was a pain unlike any other. It shook the core of my identity, just knowing I would never hear their voices again. The weight of realizing I was now an orphan cut through my heart and filled it with wave after wave of grief that I couldn't articulate to anyone. My wife Georgina carried my heart in the darkest moments of loss, but it was my sons-in-law who carried my spirit. The days before the funeral were filled with incredible anguish and all I felt was shock, but my daughters' husbands—Abraham, TJ, and Joey—stood on either side of me, lifting my arms, protecting my steps, and bringing me back to the well of healing. At the end of the week, these three men and I walked closer than we had ever walked before. God used these men to uphold my spirit beyond the pain I felt in that now moment and pulled me with them into the next moments of peace and restoration.

It would have been easy to put up a wall and hide my own pain to protect an image of strength, but it wouldn't have been genuine and my sons would have seen it. Instead, it spoke volumes to them that I was able to share my deepest pain with them, and it impacted me tremendously that God had given me sons I could entrust my heart to. That week, and the days and weeks that followed, were filled with moments of incredible leadership from this next generation of men who ministered to my now. It's one thing to share your victories with those you walk closest with, but to share your woes with those who have only seen your strength is another thing entirely.

If we're ever going to break through the rules of the now and the next to forge actual, genuine partnerships with those who've come before us, those who are beside us, and those who will go beyond us, then we need to break down the walls that isolate our pain from them. And the associated risk of vulnerability must be acknowledged and treated with care as well, so that the highway of trust continues to flow in both directions. If we can't learn to humble ourselves and work together, we'll lose more than we think.

Thankfully, the opposite is true as well. If we learn to humble ourselves, we'll gain more than we ever imagined.

Once we break the three rules and begin to bridge the generational gap, we'll see many more opportunities to keep the pathway toward one another clear. Those opportunities will come when there is an environment of love, trust, and respect being built by both the now and the next. With transparent communication, genuine appreciation, and consistent humility, we begin to build *communitas* instead of the more widely accepted *community*. *Community* refers to a people who are bonded together for self-interest. *Communitas* is a Latin word that refers to the spirit that joins people together in a common cause and mission. It's the difference between "them for me" and "me for them." Together God is calling us to break through the pursuit of community to go after the greater purpose of *communitas*.

For the first time in history, as many as five generations work side-by-side in today's workplaces, classrooms, and churches. More than ever before, the now and the next must start to take steps toward each other to close the generational gap. If we can break the rules in us that stop the generational blessing from flowing freely from the now to the next, we'll see a rise in power, authority, and influence that isn't limited to the church walls and church repertoire. It will overflow out of the church doors and into the streets, homes, schools, and offices of those who don't know God, but want to know Him. It will spill into the next generation outside of the church who don't know if there is a next step for them with God. It will change the generations yet to be born and those yet to awaken by creating a sound of convergence that the world has never heard before. It's the same sound we read about in the Bible when the now and the next stood in what God had built through both generations:

> *All the people gave a great shout, praising the LORD because the foundation of the LORD's Temple had been laid. But many of the older priests, Levites, and other leaders who had seen the first Temple wept aloud when they saw the new Temple's foundation. The others, however, were shouting for joy. The joyful shouting and weeping mingled together in a loud noise that could be heard far in the distance.* (Ezra 3:11–13)

The sound of shouting with joy for what's to come combined with the weeping of those who remember what's been can be heard far into the future. It's not the sound of one generation, but the sound of multiple generations working together to be the church that Jesus is coming back for. It's the sound of our future's future and it starts right now with you.

Rule #1: God is bigger than rules.

12

A CLEAN SLATE

"Love rules without rules."
—Italian Proverb

There a lot of things God wants to be in your life, but there are some things He never wants to be again.

The more we learn about God and the more our faith in Him grows, the less likely we are to go back to how we once saw Him. Growing in our knowledge of Him will always lead us closer to Him and further away from the rules and misconceptions of who He is that once alienated us from Him. Our newfound relationship with Him challenges us to take the limits off of Him and finally let go of old theologies, once and for all. All that you've been trying to take hold of in your life and in your relationship with Him is founded on the absolute truth that there is not a single rule that can keep you outside the door of His acceptance, favor, and promotion.

Our relationship with God will only continue to grow and develop if we make the decision to not go back to what we once believed, thought, and tolerated. Before we discovered the God who breaks the rules, most of us lived with a limited image, relationship, and perspective of Him. We held on to the wrong contexts about Him. But now that you fully grasp that God came into your life to free you from limiting theologies about Him, His grace, and His favor, you gain the confidence to move on to new conversations and experiences with Him. This new epiphany of truth and grace leads you to be able to say with Paul:

> *We know very well that we are not set right with God by rule-keeping but only through personal faith in Jesus Christ. How do we know? We tried it—and we had the best system of rules the world has ever seen!.... I tried keeping rules and working my head off to please God, and it didn't work.* (Galatians 2:16, 19 MSG)

The truth is that if rules didn't work back then for Paul, they're not going to work now. However you saw God before, I believe that's not how you see Him anymore. Maybe your original perspective of Him was similar to a lifeless myth or religious idol. Maybe you saw Him standing stoic behind a system of rules and regulations. Maybe you saw Him through the lens of a brief nostalgic memory from when you were younger. Or maybe you saw Him as a distant father who was detached from your life. All that has changed. Now you can see Him for who He truly is and what He's done so you could know Him personally.

It is my prayer that this journey through the paradoxes of God has given you a greater depth of understanding and knowledge of Him that will enlarge your revelation and relationship with Him. It's my belief and prayer that today you will stand a little taller, walk a little stronger, and see a little further because you have broken through the limiting images of who He is to you.

Now it's up to you and me to stay free from the limiting rules of the past.

Where we once held to a pattern of rejecting and limiting God, we can now begin to establish a new pattern with Him that enlarges our life to fit a reflection of a mighty God. All of the can'ts and won'ts that were part of your vocabulary can now be replaced with *He can* and *He will*. His patterns become the guidelines for new patterns that lead you not to perfection, but toward progression. Instead of feeling as though you can't ever make a mistake, you see the benefits and growth that comes from allowing Him to correct, adjust, and redirect your steps. Rather than living afraid and isolated from a God that you're unsure of, you can now walk confidently into the future He's written for you, even if that means a different path than you originally thought. Regardless of where He leads you, you know that the end of the road isn't more rules or barriers between you and God. It's a wide, open, spacious life that pushes you forward.

> ## Rather than living afraid and isolated from a God that you're unsure of, you can now walk confidently into the future He's written for you.

By now you've figured out and accepted that following rules doesn't equate to following Him. Your freedom was purchased by relationship for relationship, not by relationship for religious rules. And He didn't do it so that you could remain a slave to a new set of rules in the future. If we will approach each day with a sense of freedom, we will make the choice over and over again to go forward instead of backward. Freedom is a simple concept in theory but much more complicated in practice. There will be moments when you'll be tempted to go back just because it's easier to go back to what you've known than to go forward and rebuild a new belief system on fresh faith. There will be times when you'll regret starting this journey to know the God who breaks the rules because it's vulnerable, exposing, and revealing. But if you'll walk your freedom out all the way through, it will be rewarding in ways you never imagined.

He will begin to show you that it's not just hwo you see Him that's changed. You've changed too. And this new you is not founded in one moment, one breakthrough, or one revelation. You're constantly evolving and progressing as God can now reveal more and more of who He is to you.

God, who was once seemingly distant and detached, now invades every detail of your life to bring resolution, peace, and purpose. No longer does the wall of human inadequacy loom over your future. Gone is the spirit of insecurity and fear that you're unworthy, unqualified, and unredeemable. Erased are the notions that society's rules mimic heaven's. Now a life sketched out of imperfections creates opportunities for the liberation of others. The future now becomes a clean slate without boundaries, borders, and limitations, and nothing stands between you and the unrestricted life found in Christ.

No longer does the wall of human inadequacy loom over your future.

NEW WRITING ON THE WALL

So now what?

You've traded in the rules that you no longer need for a blank slate—what next? The freedom of learning to know God in a new dimension and facet gives you a new opportunity to experience parts of His character, heart, and nature that you've never known before. Instead of a set of rules that someone has established for you, as you get closer to Him, you begin to be part of the conversation with Him that reveals and defines new boundary lines for your life.

Growing in your relationship with Him creates a framework of progressive revelation that teaches you what hurts Him, angers Him, frustrates Him, pleases Him, and honors Him. When you know Him intimately enough to know the intricacies of His heart you naturally begin to make decisions that reflect His heart. His love for you begins to rule over you and lead you out of the wilderness of rules. Instead of opting to not have any rules, it becomes an instinctive response for you to establish boundaries that protect your relationship with Him. Not out of obligation, but as a demonstration of your personal relationship with the God who exists beyond rules.

Through intentionality, our life begins to be indicative of an ever-growing, ever-learning, and ever-advancing relationship, not only with Him but with everyone who is coming into their own revelation of a God who breaks the rules for them. The larger your world gets, the more you want others to experience the height, width, breadth, and length of your God. Going forward in your newly discovered revelations of Him will never be a walk alone. It will inevitably include people along the way who are also discovering the largeness and vastness of God's presence in *their* lives. Revelation will always beget revelation. As you stay in awe of who God is, you become passionate about introducing others to a God that doesn't fit their mold. You feel obligated out of gratitude to not allow anyone in your presence to live with a marginalized image of His presence.

Your clean slate begins to include others who have lived with a limited understanding of Him but who are now being introduced to the God who breaks the rules through your example, testimony, and passion. Some will be drawn to have their own personal encounter with Him. Others will despise you, criticize you, and argue with you because their revelation of God is not the same as yours. Either way, God will use your life and your revelation of Him to start them off on their own crossroads of faith. The world is desperate to know Him for themselves, even if they can't articulate it on their own. The condition and heartbreak of humanity that exists in our everyday life gives ample testimony to our need for *more of God* and *less of rules*. Just as God brought you on this journey of discovery with Him, allow your life to do the same in someone else.

The beautiful part about God is that He *wants* you to know every part of Him. He's not trying to hide behind rules and statutes that keep pertinent parts of Himself hidden from you. He created you and me in His image so we could understand and emulate that image to the world around us. When the image we portray of Him is contrary to who He truly is, it pushes people away, and that is never his desire.

I challenge you to live a life with God that is so contrary to the popular beliefs of Him that it forces you to have to explain how and why God moves in your life so unorthodoxically, unconventionally, and unexplainably. Let people be so perplexed about God's favor and promotion on your life that they want to try and understand how your relationship with Him works. Your faith in a God who breaks the rules is like a front page story in the news every time He works in a way that other people don't understand. They'll want to know why God works in paradoxes in your life and how they can see Him do the same in theirs. Even if they aren't ready to believe in a rule-breaking God yet, they will still want to know what inspires you to believe in Him. No one wants to be deceived or left out of the loop on something they don't know. This is why Adam and Eve were tempted to sin—they desired more knowledge. They wanted to know what God knew. They wanted to be able to say there was nothing they didn't know. In the same way, people will be drawn to you because they want to know what you know.

God withholds nothing from us so that we can begin to live withholding nothing from Him.

I have often wondered why God would choose to leave all the aspects of David's life—the good, the bad, and the ugly—in print for us to read in Scripture. If God forgave him, why did He need to include it all? I believe it's because the more we know of the story, the more we know of the Author. If we didn't know the details of David's life that included every aspect of his journey with Him, we wouldn't even begin to know a God who isn't afraid to use unlikely people, and work in unlikely ways, to reach unlikely people.

God does the same thing through the story He is writing in your life and mine. He's letting the world around you see the times when you've run from Him, run toward Him, and run for Him so that they can see the multidimensional facets of who He is in your life. You wouldn't be able to reap a benefit from a story that started wrong and ended well without knowing everything that happened in between. But God withholds nothing from us so that we can begin to live withholding nothing from Him.

BEYOND RELIGION

Derick grew up believing God wanted very little to do with him and, in all honesty, the feeling was mutual. His parents were avid believers in a religion that only left him with more questions than answers, but he obeyed them and followed them to church every week. However, as a young adult, he decided he was done with the religious traditions that didn't lead him any closer to God. He couldn't understand why he was required to do certain things when he didn't have any real relationship with God. He had seen too much proof in the men and women around him in church for years that religion didn't change your life. They were still just the same. Completely convinced that church and religion was nothing more than a waste of time filled with senseless traditions, rituals, and rules, he convinced his parents to let him stop going with them. He was so determined to say goodbye to religion that he made a pact with his best friend to never set foot in a church again. He said goodbye to God and that part of his life and moved on.

Four years later he met a young woman at work that changed everything. They became friends, and at work she shared with him her newfound relationship with God with more passion and joy than he'd ever seen. She had a way of expressing her faith in God that made him think she had what God must have wanted everyone to have. He still wasn't convinced he wanted anything to do with her God or church, but he loved to hear her stories of services, worship practice, Bible studies, and more. She opened a new aspect of God to him that he had never encountered before. For over a year their friendship grew into more and with each of her stories, he began to see a God that he was willing to get to know better.

His first experience with our church wasn't at one of our church services at all. Georgina and I were teaching a small group about relationships, and Derick agreed to attend the small group with the young woman. Some said he only agreed to go because he wanted to pursue a relationship with her beyond friendship, and they would probably have been right. But in God's perfect, unorthodox plan, He was using her to call Derick back to Him.

Derick started coming every week to our Bible study and gradually began to become more open to the possibility of one day visiting us on a Sunday. Six months later, he had accepted Christ, experienced salvation for the first time, and was attending regularly. At that time our church was still growing and beginning to need a staff. I learned that Derick had some experience in computers so I invited him to start volunteering on staff as a graphic designer. He became our official graphic designer and the fourth member of our staff. God began using this unqualified, barely-saved young man to help build our church. As he grew in his relationship with God, Derick's life radically changed. He married that young girl whose stories of faith had led him to Christ, became a father, and transformed into one of our core leaders. Today he is one of our assistant pastors and committed to helping those who have completely walked away from God find their way back. God took this man who walked away from God, broke his rules and excuses, repurposed his life, and called him to be a billboard for a paradoxical relationship with God.

Maybe you're in the same place Derick was. Maybe you're ready to walk away from God because you've never experienced Him beyond religion. Maybe you have already said goodbye to Him and moved on. But just like with Derick, God will send an unlikely person in your life to introduce you to a God much larger than you've ever known. And He may very well bring you back to Him and the local church through an unconventional door like a small group. Derick's story is one of the reasons we believe the life of the church is in the life groups, or small groups, that we hold every week. They're places where we can bring the church and God to the people that need Him most, but don't want to come the traditional way. When we don't limit the ways God can reach people, we give Him room to extend our walls and create doors through every aspect of our lives and ministry.

The good life God has promised you and me is not just found in encountering the God who breaks the rules. It's unlocked when we adjust our lives to follow His paradoxical methods, obey His unorthodox plans, and find our new identity in this newfound call and purpose. Whatever chapter you think you've closed in your life with God, never underestimate His ability to call you home. And not just you, but also those who've given up and need to hear your stories of faith with passion and joy that leads them to want to experience the same for themselves. Using you and me to be His representatives to the world is an absurd plan for evangelism since we are filled with imperfections that don't reflect His perfection. Nevertheless, God would rather tell the world about His grace for our imperfections than about His standard of perfection that we could never meet without Him.

In ourselves we are the least likely, least qualified, and least obvious choice to change the world for Him, but then again, so were His disciples. The disciples were just twelve ordinary men who followed an extraordinary Savior. When Jesus died and the mission left behind was to evangelize the world, these guys would not have been our first choice. As a whole, they were intolerant, selfishly ambitious, materialistic, secretive, impulsive, intense, and even negative and pessimistic. On top of all that, they were slow learners and spiritually immature. But they were also teachable and believed who Jesus was even when they didn't believe in His methods. They loved and admired Jesus personally. They wanted to be the right men despite the fact that they knew they fell short. What made them the right choice is what makes us the right choice today—a love for Jesus beyond personal devotion to any and every other cause. The only qualification that truly qualified them to change the world after His resurrection was that they loved Him more than anything and everything else. More than Scripture, more than a church, more than doctrines, and more than any religious cause.

They loved all of those things deeply and profoundly, but only because *they loved Him first.*

Your love for Him first and foremost is the key to loving everything He loves and entering into the good life that comes from living in His abundance. When you love Him, you will naturally love Scripture because you'll want to know His words, His thoughts, His plans, and His truth. When you love Him, you will love His church because you'll want to be around other people who love Him and you'll want to be part of the bride He's coming back for. When you love Him, you'll want to know His doctrines so that you can be grounded in His principles even as His methods change. And when you love Him, you'll want to take on His cause as your own. Loving Him and loving all the things He loves becomes synonymous as your life becomes large enough to encompass all that He wants to do through it.

Instead of cutting your life into separate sections, with God, church, and ministry being just parts of a whole, your entire life now flows from Him to everything else. When this becomes how you process what is your priority, you walk with greater strength, greater power, and greater authority.

WORKING THROUGH PAST, PRESENT, AND FUTURE

At the end of his life, David knew what it was like to put God first and he knew what it was like to put himself first. He had lived going after what God wanted and he had lived going after what he wanted. He had known what it means to experience God's blessing and His consequences. He had lived in the liberty and freedom of walking close to God and he had lived in the limitations of walking far from God. After all his seasons of coming and going with God, he comes back desiring nothing more than Him:

> LORD, teach me how you want me to live. Do this so that I will depend on you, my faithful God. Give me a heart that doesn't want anything more than to worship you.   (Psalm 86:11 NIRV)

It's almost as though David is saying, "OK God, let's be honest. I've done it my way for a while and wanted way too many things for myself and now I need you to teach me *again* how to do it Your way. Then I won't want anything else but You." He's at a point in his life where all he wants is to come back to a place where God is first.

Haven't we all gotten to the same place at one point in our lives? Maybe you, too, know what it's like to live with rules and you know what it's like to live without rules. Maybe you know what it's like to go after what God wants and what it's like to go after what you want. Or maybe you know what it feels like to experience the goodness of God's blessing and what it's like to walk in the painful reality of His consequences. And now you're at the point where you're just ready to start over and let God show you again how He wants you to live so you'll want only Him again. Remember that David knew God very well before he wrote this psalm. He's not asking Him to teach him something new as much as he's asking Him to teach him something again in a new way. God will always bring us back to a place where we realize again and again that a life with Him is the only thing we truly need.

Living the good life in God is being able to take the wisdom from the past and apply it to the realities of the present so you can be better prepared for what's to come. It's looking back at the rules that once confined you so you can make different choices today to be able to live free for the rest of your life. It's honoring how the past positioned you for today while keeping your eyes on the future. It's being able to see what you did right yesterday so you can be encouraged today to keep going after a better tomorrow.

When you give God permission to work through your past, present, and future, He uses the paradox of His omnipresence to break the rules that prevent you from living out your future. It's His ability to use the things from your past to work out who you are in the present that secures your future. We aren't privileged to see how our past, present, and future mirror one another, so we're more tempted to give up when we can't see the light at the end of the tunnel. But God breaks the rules of how time works, either for or against you, to remind you that He chose you and called you because of His love that existed before time ever began.

His ability to use the things from your past to work out who you are in the present secures your future.

While the world may have a variety of images, theologies, and personas to explain and describe God, He is more concerned about how *you* see Him. He is willing to push through every religious obstacle between you and Him to call you from the soiled, unqualified, and unlikely place of your life to anoint you, sanctify you, and vindicate you so you will place your theological beliefs in Him alone. He is committed to exposing, confronting, and abolishing the rules that have separated you from Him, even if that means He has to expose the places in you that are stuck in religious routines. Your life is no different than David's. God will do anything and everything to call you from the field, anoint you to the table of promotion, and guide you through the process of stepping into the lineage of royalty that exists in you because of Him. He won't give up or stop pursuing you until you finally know, believe, and accept the paradoxes of His love and grace that prove He is the God who breaks the rules for you.

WHEN RULES NO LONGER RULE YOU

The dictionary defines the word *paradox* as a seemingly absurd or self-contradictory statement or proposition that when investigated or explained may prove to be well-founded or true.

Through the life of the biblical David and the stories of modern-day Davids that are being raised all over the world, God is proving that every absurd and self-contradictory statement about Him being the God who breaks the rules are in fact true. Through the paradoxical stories, we learn there is absolute truth in the fact that He will call the unqualified from the most unlikely of places to position, promote, and favor them.

In fact, we know that God broke environmental, cultural, and societal rules to reveal Himself to humanity. We can know with certainty that it is in God's nature to sanctify the most soiled people through the purity of grace that came through His Son. All of this truth comes to us today to help give us the greater revelation of who He was, is, and will forever be—the God who breaks the rules.

Accepting the truth of God's paradoxes isn't just knowledge. It is a greater revelation of His nature, character, and plan for your life. It's the revelation of His authority over and above all man-made, hindering rules. It's a revelation that pushes you, propels you, and impels you to believe that the same power to live beyond rules exists in you, too.

It's time to break the unspoken and spoken rules that have limited your faith in God, in yourself, and in your future, by believing more in what *He* says than what *rules* say. It's time to believe in God's ability to see you, truly see you, through His lens and His vantage point instead of believing the lies that have been formed by what was done in the past. It's time to let yourself see and experience the parts of God that have been hidden behind a shroud of religious rules, regulations, and standards that only speak the language of perfection or punishment.

It's time to begin a new chapter in your relationship with God that is no longer filled with pages and pages of rules.

The slate is now clean, the pages are now empty, and the freedom to live free from stifling, limiting rules is ready to be penned by the paradoxes of God. His hand of grace and truth leads you by the hand into the unknown path of your future. And while it still may be unknown to you, it has always been known by the God who has known you since before you were even born. He's the God who sent His Son to step out of heaven so you could enter in. He's the God who paid a price so great you would see the greatness in you. He's the God who opens wide His arms to redeem your past, present, and future.

And He's the God who broke the rules to do it.

It's time to begin a new chapter
in your relationship with God
that is no longer filled with
pages and pages of rules.

ACKNOWLEDGMENTS

Above all, to Jesus, who broke the rules for me and continues to break my rules every day. I could never have imagined all that I have seen, experienced, and lived, but it was always a part of Your plan for my life. I'm eternally grateful.

To my faithful, beautiful, and incredible bride, Georgina, who has believed with me, built with me, and broken rules with me to see hearts turned since day one. Excited for all that awaits us in the future. I will always love you, Georgi!

To my greatest gifts—Selena, Joey, Crystal, Abraham, Carissa, TJ, Alexis, Angel, Miracle Joy, JJ, and Gracin—who have all brought me a depth of joy that could never be expressed in words. I see the call of God on each of you and am proud of your unconventional passion and pursuit after Jesus. The world is waiting for you.

To my brothers, sisters, and family, who have been a constant source of love and loyalty. More than ever before, I am proud of who we are, who we represent, and who we are becoming. Because of each of you, the De La Mora family has a legacy that will last a lifetime.

To my pastors, Art and Kuna Sepúlveda, who have never wavered in their love, belief, and covering over me. Thank you for every phone call, every word of wisdom, and every prayer. Your voices continue to remain the ones that make the difference in my life.

To our amazing Cornerstone Church family, who have chosen to live from the paradoxes of His grace and truth to see the vision and mission of

Cornerstone come to pass. Through your stories, the world will know God's uncommon, unorthodox, and undeniable love.

To our wonderful staff, assistant pastors, and Team 12 Leaders, who have laid down their lives to honor the past while remaining ferociously loyal to the future. Pastor Georgina and I thank God for your families, your leadership, and your willingness to keep growing with us! Our best is still yet to come!

To Leticia Ventura, for being the brilliant human hard drive who can assimilate and conjugate my thoughts in ways that only God could have ordained. And thank you to the entire Ventura family—Derick, David, Bella, Ava, and Ella—for choosing every day to be a family that keeps saying yes.

To the entire staff at Whitaker House, who believed in the God who breaks the rules and who believed in me personally. Thank you for being editors and publishers who truly want to glorify God through print.

ABOUT THE AUTHOR

Sergio De La Mora is the visionary founder and pastor of Cornerstone Church of San Diego, ranked one of the fastest growing churches in America with multiple satellite campuses. Called the "Turn Around Specialist," he has influenced a multi-generational and multiethnic community in both English and Spanish for almost twenty years. His passion and vision to plant churches with the purpose of reaching new territory for Christ led him to launch several satellite campuses.

Sergio is also founder of The Heart Revolution Conference, which gathers well-known thought leaders from all over the nation to revolutionize the hearts of the next generation. This international conference has now grown annually to become one of the most highly anticipated leadership gatherings in America. He is cofounder of the Turning the Hearts Center, a nonprofit organization designed to empower youth and families and restore family unity and self-sufficiency through a variety of programs and support resources, including a Food Distribution Center that feeds hundreds of families in the community every month.

Sergio's inspirational first book, *The Heart Revolution*, was released in both English and Spanish. Sergio lives in San Diego with his wife, Georgina, and their six daughters.